REVELATION DREAMS
PROPHETIC VISIONS OF
HOPE AND WARNING
BY
DONNA LISA DAVIS

Published by Donna Lisa Davis

Atlantic Beach, FL

First Edition ISBN 979-8-218-72778-9

Cover Design by Donna Lisa Davis

Contact Information:

Email: ddavisprophetic@yahoo.com

TikTok: @donnalisa385

YouTube: @donnalisa385

Instagram: @donnalisa385

Printed in the United States of America First Edition

Dedication

To the One who reveals mysteries, our Lord Jesus Christ, the Alpha and the Omega, who was, and is, and is to come. May these revelations stir hearts to repentance, draw believers closer to Him, and prepare His people for the coming of His Kingdom.

"The secret things belong to the Lord our God, but those things which are revealed belong to us and to our children forever, that we may do all the words of this law." (Deuteronomy 29:29), NKJV

He Who Speaks Through Dreams

Since the beginning of time, God has spoken to His people in various ways: through His Word, through His prophets, and through dreams and visions. These divine messages often carry profound warnings, encouragement, and revelation.

"For God may speak in one way, or in another, yet man does not perceive it. In a dream, in a vision of the night, when deep sleep falls upon men, while slumbering on their beds, then He opens the ears of men, and seals their instruction." (Job 33:14-16), NKJV.

Let us pray:
Heavenly Father, we come before You in the name of Jesus Christ, asking that You open the spiritual eyes and ears of every person who reads this book. Let them see and hear through Your Spirit, gaining understanding and wisdom from Your Word. May the messages within these pages pierce the hearts of those reading, turning them away from their wicked ways and leading them to true repentance.

Lord, may they cling to Your Word, walking in obedience and holding it close to their hearts. Let this book serve as a beacon, drawing many into Your light and truth. We ask this in the mighty name of Jesus Christ, our Lord and Savior.

Table Of Contents

Chapter 1 1

Concentration Camp 1

Chapter 2 15

Bride in Waiting...15

Chapter 3 23

The Dream: Demons In the Church.......................................23

Chapter 4 28

Dream of the White House and the Sealed Door.................28

Chapter 5 35

The Prophetic Dream of the Multitude in White..................35

Shadows In the Park..36

The House of Old Bones..41

Chapter 6 47

The White Horse Dream/ Revelation Dream 47

The Black Horse Dream and the Pouring of God's Spirit...........51

Chapter 7..58

The Fiery Call Dream Revelation 58

The War Cry: A Prophetic Call to Intercede for Israel...............63

Chapter 8 66

The Dream of the Invasion and the Hidden Covering...................66

Chapter 9 86

The Song of the Innocent 86

Chapter 10..90

The Desolation of Moscow, Russia- A Prophetic Warning Dream
....90

Chapter 11 103

The Royal Road: A Sword for the Called103Chapter 12 108

When Your Feet Get Wet 108

Chapter 13 112

The Heavenly Construction Dream 112

Chapter 14 118

The Garden Encounter A Dream from 1985 118

Why didn't they save Jesus? 125

Chapter 15 134

Under His Wings A Dream of Covering and Calling 138

Awake in the Coffin 146

Spiritual Insight and Interpretation 147

The Sky Rolled Back 151

The Anointed Outpouring Over My Family 154

The Two Generals and the Spirit Behind Power 159

Do You Know What You Think You Know? 164

Acknowledgments 171

Author 172

Author Quote: 173

Chapter 1

Concentration Camp

Dream Date: June 26, 2024

A Silent Observer

June 26, 2024, 6:00 a.m.

The day was bright, as if the sun had chosen to show every corner of the earth. I found myself sitting on the familiar porch of my grandmother's house, a place of warmth and memory. But this time, something was different, I was not there. I was observing, more spirit than flesh, hovering as though caught between two worlds. The air felt heavy, and I knew, even in this otherworldly state, that I was about to witness something I would never forget.

From my place on the porch, I could see a young man standing nearby, alone yet somehow uneasy, as though he sensed something I could not. Suddenly, a woman approached him. She was holding a clipboard, her movements quick and efficient. She didn't look at him as one might look at a friend, but rather as a person assessing a task. She was petitioning, knocking on doors, handing out leaflets. But this was no ordinary job offer. I have an opportunity," she said, her voice carrying an edge of persuasion that sounded practiced, almost rehearsed. She paused, waiting for him to respond. The young man hesitated, his face unreadable "It's a paid position," she continued, "but there's a catch. You'll have to wear a striped suit. It's part of the uniform."

I could feel his curiosity turning into caution, the word catch settling heavily in the air. "A striped suit?" he echoed, his voice filled with a mixture of curiosity and distress," yes, she replied, unfazed. "You'd be required to administer shots to prisoners, as part of containment, she left it at that, offering no further explanation, and yet, in the stillness of that moment, it felt as if something had already shifted.

A Step into Darkness

In an instant, the scene shifted. Suddenly, we were no longer at my grandmother's house but in a new place, a place that held a familiarity. It was Montgomery, Alabama, I recognized the white Capitol building gleaming against the sky. But beside it, there loomed a prison, a structure that, on the outside, appeared sturdy and impassive, yet on the inside was filled with turmoil. The young man walked forward, and although I was only an observer, I felt compelled to follow. I could sense his dread as he stepped past the gates and entered what looked like a camp. Unlike a traditional prison, this place housed not just criminals but entire families. Mothers, fathers, children—all were confined together, their faces etched with fear, sickness, and resignation.

Chaos reigned, spilling over from every corner, and a sense of darkness seemed to seep into every soul within those walls. It didn't take long to see that something dreadful was happening here. People were lining up, their faces pale and drawn, their bodies trembling. They were waiting for a shot, the same shot the woman had mentioned. But as I looked closer, I realized that this shot was not a cure; it was a sentence.

Those who received it collapsed soon after, their bodies crumbling like fragile paper. There was no cure here, no safety, only despair.

The Flight to Freedom

Desperation began to fill the air, an unspoken urgency passing through the crowd. The young man, seeing the fate that awaited him, turned to flee, his heart pounding with a fear that rippled through my own spirit. Yet, even as he moved, he was caught, a man in a black suit, neither a police officer nor military but an authoritative figure, grabbed him and brought him back, trapping him once more. Nearby, I saw a family attempting to escape. The father, a man with a strong presence, perhaps a leader in his own right, was instructing his wife to make a run for it, to take the children and flee to the car while he created a diversion.

They had a convertible, a small sign of the life they had once lived, of wealth or privilege that meant little in this new reality. The woman held her children close, one on each side, her eyes brimming with terror. She took them to the car, glancing back just once at her husband, who nodded as if to say, Go. I'll find you. The young man, watching this unfold, begged the woman for refuge. She hesitated; clearly torn between her own safety and the compassion she felt for this stranger. Finally, she relented, allowing him to climb in beside her. Together, they sped off, the boundaries of the camp disappearing into the distance.

Hope in a Drawing

The scene shifted again, and I found myself in a new place, a place of refuge. It could have been a hotel, a house, some hidden sanctuary, a place untouched by the darkness that had gripped the camp. Here, the air was different, filled with a quiet peace that seemed foreign after all I had just seen. The young man, safe at last, took a moment to comfort the little girl from the family. She was frightened, clutching a doll in one hand, her face pale, and her eyes wide with fear.

Kneeling down, he took out a piece of paper and began to draw. He sketched a picture of the family, standing together, with new friends and even a dog at their side. Handing her the drawing, he spoke softly: "This is your new place, a different life, with new friends. You're safe here." The girl's face softened, her eyes filling with something that looked like hope. In that small drawing, he had given her something priceless, a vision of a future untouched by darkness.

A Vision of Spiritual Warning

As I reflected on the dream's details, I felt compelled to look at it in light of scripture, seeking to understand its message not only as a warning but also as a call for spiritual renewal. What I had witnessed in the dream seemed to echo the kind of visions given to prophets—moments where God unveils a reality unseen to the physical eye, yet vital for the spirit to comprehend. One passage that came to mind was in the book of Joel, where God speaks about revealing Himself through dreams and visions.

And it shall come to pass afterward, that I will pour out my Spirit on all flesh; your sons and your daughters shall prophesy, your old men shall dream dreams, your young men shall see visions. (Joel 2:28, NKJV).

This dream felt like a fulfillment of Joel's words. I felt as if I were being shown what might happen if we continued down a path away from God. It was a message meant not just for me but for all who would hear it.

The Young Man's Dilemma and the Striped Suit

In my dream, I observed the young man as he stood, undecided, before the woman with the clipboard. Her offer held both promise and peril. The striped suit, while just a uniform, seemed to symbolize a false sense of freedom, blending him with the prisoners he was tasked to serve. It reminded me of the subtle ways in which we can be led into compromising situations without realizing the consequences.

For if a man think himself to be something, when he is nothing, he deceived himself. (Galatians 6:3, KJV)

The young man's decision to accept this job, despite the unease in his heart, reflected how we sometimes deceive ourselves into thinking we can tread dangerous ground without consequence. In accepting the position, he became part of the same captivity he was supposed to administer, a warning to us about the dangers of complacency and compromise.

(Ephesians 4:27 NKJV), says, nor give place to the devil. [give no opportunity to him].

Lord, I ask you to help us keep the doors to our heart and soul closed to the devil!

A Prison of Families and the Cry for Deliverance

Inside the camp, I saw families imprisoned, torn from their former lives, and stripped of freedom. It reminded me of the Israelites under Egyptian bondage, suffering and longing for deliverance. Like the Israelites, these people had been confined by forces beyond their control, placed in a system that treated them as less than human. The camp echoed the heartache of a society in chains, crying out for release. The Spirit of the Lord God is upon me, because the Lord has anointed me to preach good tiding to the poor; He has sent me to heal the brokenhearted, to proclaim liberty to the captives, and the opening of the prison to those who are bound. **(Isaiah 61:1, NKJV)**

Isaiah's words remind us that God's heart is with those who suffer and that His will is to set them free. Seeing the families confined in the camp, I felt an urgency for repentance, knowing that without a return to God, we risk creating our own prisons—spiritually, morally, and even physically **(Job 11:13-18, NKJV).** If you would prepare your heart, and stretch out your hands toward him; if iniquity were in your hands, and you put it far away, and you will not let the wickedness dwell in your tent; then surely you could lift up your face without spot; Yes, you could be steadfast, and not fear; Because you would forget your misery, and remember it as waters that have passed away, and your life would be brighter than noonday. Though you were dark, you would be like the morning. And you will be secure, because there is hope; Yes, you would dig around and take rest in safety.

The Shots of Containment and the Illusion of Control

The shots, intended to "contain" the disease, only brought more suffering, ending lives instead of healing them. It became clear that the solution imposed on these people was not for their good. Instead, it was an illusion of control, a remedy that held death instead of life. This scene spoke to the consequences of relying on solutions born out of fear rather than faith.

There is a way that seems right to a man, but its end is the way to death. (Proverbs 14:12, NKJV).

This proverb warns against leaning on human wisdom without divine guidance. The shots symbolized the ways we can create solutions to problems without seeking God's direction, often leading to unintended consequences that harm rather than heal.

(Matthew 7:13-14 NKJV). Says, "Enter by the narrow gate; for wide is the gate and broad is the way that leads to destruction, and there are many who go in by it. Because narrow is the gate and difficult is the way which leads to life, and there are few who find it.

Jesus is presenting two paths, one that leads to destruction and one that leads to life. The path to destruction is the way of self-gratification, while the path to life is narrow way that requires admitting a need for help from Jesus Christ. Let us walk down the narrow path to life.

Escape and the Cost of Freedom

As I watched the family's escape, I felt the weight of their struggle. The father sacrificed his safety so that his wife and children might reach freedom, reflecting a love that sought to protect others even at great personal cost. His courage reminded me of the selfless love Christ showed in laying down His life for humanity's sake.

Greater love has no one than this, than to lay down one's life for his friends. (John 15:13, NKJV).

The family's escape represented the cost of freedom, the courage needed to break free from chains, and the willingness to risk everything for the sake of those we love. The father's actions echoed Christ's love, a reminder that true freedom often requires sacrifice. **(Acts 17:24-27 NKJV)**. God, who made the world and everything in it, since He is the Lord of heaven and earth, does not dwell in temples made with hands. Nor is He worshiped with men's hands, as though He needed anything, since He gives to all life, breath, and all things. And He has made from one blood every nation of men to dwell on all the face on the earth and has determined their preappointed times and the boundaries of their dwellings, so that they should seek the lord, in the hope that they might grope for Him and find Him, though He is not far from each of us.

Prayer

Heavenly father, thank you for loving me. Help me love others the way you love me. Let me find love in the things of heaven. Keep me from loving the world. Let me have love in my heart.

Take all selfishness away from me and let me have love for others. Amen!

A Place of Refuge

When the young man and the family finally reached a place of safety, the atmosphere changed. It was a quiet sanctuary, a stark contrast to the chaos of the camp. Here, the fear and tension melted away, replaced by peace and relief. In this safe haven, I saw a glimpse of God's promise to shelter His people in times of trouble.

You are my hiding place; you shall preserve me from trouble; You shall surround me with songs of deliverance." (Psalm 32:7, NKJV).

This moment of refuge was a reminder that no matter the turmoil around us, God offers a place of safety for those who seek Him. It is in His presence that we find rest, healing, and the strength to face whatever lies ahead.

The Lord also will be a refuge for the oppressed, a refuge in times of trouble. (Psalm 9:9, NKJV).

Psalm 9 is about how the Lord never forsakes or forgets those who belong to him. Because of this, God's people should praise Him. Bless the Lord that blesses us. Psalm 9 is very powerful, it teaches us.

God's relationship with his people: God's help is given to those who have a relationship with him, have faith in him, and seek him.

God's provision of Hope: God provide hope for the downcast.

God's mercy: God is merciful even in justice.

God's answer to prayer: God answers prayer and rescues those who call on him.

My fellow Saints keep your eyes on the Lord Jesus Christ! Read the word of God in the Bible it is bread alone.

The Drawing of Hope

As the young man comforted the little girl by drawing a picture of her family and friends, he showed her a vision of life beyond the camp, a new beginning. This act of compassion touched me deeply, reminding me that hope can be a powerful antidote to despair. In that simple drawing, he offered her something no one else could: a sense of peace and possibility.

For I know the thoughts that I think toward you, says the Lord, the thoughts of peace and not evil, to give you a future and hope. (Jeremiah 29:11, NKJV).

The drawing was a symbol of hope, a vision that life could be different. It reminded me that God, too, has a vision for each of us—a future that is bright, filled with His plans for our welfare, not our harm. Even in the darkest times, God's promises remain steadfast, and He continues to offer us hope.

Reflection on the Dream's Meaning

The weight of the dream pressed upon me long after I woke up, each image vivid, each detail etched into my memory. As I considered its significance, I felt a strong conviction to share this message. The dream was not merely a vision of suffering but a call to repentance, a plea for us to turn back to the ways of God before it is too late.

If my people who are called by My name will humble themselves, and pray and seek my face, and turn from their wicked ways, then I will hear from heaven, and I will forgive their sin and heal their land. (2 Chronicles 7:14, NKJV).

This verse became the heartbeat of my message. It is a reminder that God offers healing and restoration for those who seek Him, even when all seems lost. But it is a choice, a choice to humble ourselves, to repent, and to turn toward Him.

A Call to Repentance

As I sat in silence, reflecting on the dream, I felt an overwhelming sense of urgency. This vision had not come to me by chance; it was a call—a call to repentance, to realign our lives with God's will, and to turn away from the paths that would lead to destruction. I realized that this dream had revealed more than just a warning; it was a glimpse into what could happen if we continued down the path of neglecting our faith and values.

Scripture reminds us

Time and again that God's heart is filled with mercy, and He offers each of us an opportunity to return to Him. Yet, this requires humility and repentance.

Repent therefore, and be converted, that your sins may be blotted out, so that times of refreshing may come from the presence of the Lord. (Acts 3:19-20, NKJV).

The vision in my dream served as a powerful reminder of this truth. Just as the young man and the family found freedom, each of us can find spiritual freedom through repentance. By humbling ourselves and seeking God, we open ourselves to His grace and healing. In **(Acts 3:19 Peter)** challenges all to change their minds and change their courses. Not only is their sin addressed but their closed minds

A Vision for Renewal

I realized that beyond the warnings, there was also hope. God was not showing me this vision to create fear but to inspire change. Like the picture the young man drew for the little girl, God offers us a vision of a future filled with peace and promise.

For the mountains shall depart and the hills be removed, but my kindness shall not depart from you. Nor shall my covenant of peace be removed, says the Lord, who has mercy on you. (Isaiah 54:10, NKJV).

These words reminded me that no matter how dark the times may become, God's love remains steadfast. In turning back to Him, we can experience a renewal of life, a covenant of peace that He offers to all who seek His face.

(Isaiah 61:7, NKJV) Says, instead of your shame you shall have double honor, and instead of your confusion they shall rejoice in their portion. Therefore, in their land they shall possess double; Everlasting joy shall be theirs.

Prayer

Thank you, Lord, for your unconditional love & grace. Nothing can separate us from your love or snatch us from your hands. We thank you & love you for never letting us go. Amen!

A Future Filled with Hope

The final scene of the dream—of the young man drawing a picture of a new life—remains with me, a symbol of hope for what lies ahead. This dream has shown me that while there is much to be vigilant about, there is also reason to hope. God is always ready to forgive, to heal, and to renew, even in the darkest moments.

Have I not commanded you? Be strong and of good courage, do not be afraid, nor be dismayed, for the Lord your God is with you wherever you go. (Joshua 1:9, NKJV).

New Beginning

In the quietness after the dream, I felt a sense of peace. The vision had shown me what could befall a world that turns away from God, yet it had also shown me what could be if we return to Him. Like the young man and the family, each of us has a choice: to remain in captivity or to embrace the freedom God offers through faith.

I realized that this dream, this revelation, was not just a warning; it was an invitation—a call to new beginnings. The path forward requires courage and a willingness to let go of the things that hold us back, but with God, all things are possible. For those who seek Him, a brighter future awaits.

Now to Him who is able to exceedingly abundantly above all that we ask or think, according to the power that work in us, to Him be glory in the church by Christ Jesus to all generations, forever and ever! (Ephesians 3:20-21, NKJV)

As I close this dream, my prayer is that these words will touch hearts, that those who read will feel inspired to seek God, to repent, and to pursue the future He has planned for us—a future filled with His love, protection, and guidance.

Chapter 2

Bride in Waiting

Dream Date: April 23, 2024

I had a vivid dream I was standing in an empty church on a bright, clear day. There was a sense of calm and purity in the air, and sunlight filtered through the windows, casting a warm glow over the sanctuary. In front of me stood a bride, dressed in white, radiant, and beautiful, yet oddly distant. She wasn't in the main part of the church where one might expect a bride to be. Instead, she stood at the back, near the kitchen.

Let us be glad and rejoice and give Him glory, For the marriage of the Lamb has come, and His wife has made herself ready. (Revelation 19:7, NKJV).

Here, Revelation speaks of a bride prepared for her groom. But in this dream, she was waiting, not at the altar, but in the background. Was she truly ready for her Bridegroom?

A Bride Without a Bridegroom

I looked at her, puzzled, and wondered aloud, "Where is your bridegroom? Why are you here, in the back of the church?" She only looked out the window, silent, waiting for someone or something beyond what I could see. I felt a sense of urgency, wondering how to move her to the front of the church.

Then the kingdom of heaven shall be likened to ten virgins who took their lamps and went out to meet the bridegroom. (Matthew 25:1, NKJV).

In the parable of the ten virgins, the bridesmaids were waiting for the groom, but only those who were prepared went into the wedding feast. The others were left out, not ready when he arrived. This dream was a reminder: readiness is more than standing still; it's active, prepared waiting.

Prayer

Heavenly Father, as I actively wait on your perfect timing and plans for my life, I pray that even in this season of waiting, I may be a radiant beacon of your love to those around me. Let my words be kind, my actions be gracious, and my spirit be filled with the light of your presence, so that others may see a glimpse of your goodness through me. Grant me the strength to persevere in faith, to trust in your faithfulness, and to shine brightly for you, even during uncertainty. May my life be a testament to your hope, and may your glory be revealed through my steadfast waiting. In Jesus Christ Mighty Name, Amen,

The Kitchen of Preparation

In the dream, the bride was standing near the kitchen, a place of preparation, but she was not yet in the sanctuary. She seemed almost out of place, like she was waiting for permission or for someone to tell her it was time.

Christ also loved the church and gave himself up for her, that he might sanctify and cleanse her with the washing of water by the word. (Ephesians 5:25-26, NKJV).

The bride in this vision seemed ready but hesitated to step forward. This place of "preparation" reflected how the church is called to be sanctified, washed, and fully presented, without spot or blemish. Yet she wasn't quite there, as if something held her back.

Prayer

Heavenly father, we pray for your God's Spirit and power would fill the church and all believers. Fill us with the power of your Holy Spirit on this day. Fill us with your joy, your wisdom, and with constant reminders that Your Presence will go with us, and you will give us rest. Thank you that you came to give new life, peace, hope, and joy to your children we pray this prayer in The Mighty Name of our Lord Jesus Christ. Amen.

The Symbol of the Window

The bride's gaze was fixed outside, looking longingly out the window. Was she waiting, perhaps, for a sign or a glimpse of the bridegroom's approach?

So, Christ was offered once to bear the sins of many. To those who eagerly wait for Him He will appear a second time, apart from sins, for salvation. (Hebrews 9:28, NKJV).

Her stance by the window captured an expectant heart, watching and longing for her Savior. It was a call for the church to be ever watchful, looking for Christ's return with steadfast hope.

Prayer

Heavenly Father,

We come before You with reverence, acknowledging You as the One who calls us to live in readiness for the return of Your Son, our Bridegroom. Lord, You have chosen us as the bride of Christ, and You desire that we be vigilant, prepared, and devoted, waiting eagerly for the day we will be united with You. Amen.

A Bride in the Background

She wasn't at the altar where a bride traditionally stands, but waiting in a hidden place, almost as if she wasn't ready to step forward.

Therefore, you also be ready, for the Son of Man is coming at an hour you do not expect. (Matthew 24:44, NKJV)

There's a sense in this dream that the church is sometimes in the "back," not fully occupying the place she is meant to, perhaps waiting but unsure. This is a reminder that readiness is about positioning ourselves at the forefront, prepared to meet Christ.

Prayer

Heavenly Father,

We pray, O Lord, that You would awaken in Your church a spirit of watchfulness. Stir our hearts to be sensitive to Your guidance. May we not be caught unaware or distracted by cares of this world but be steadfast, rooted deeply in Your Word, discerning the times and season as you reveal them to us. Amen

The Call to Move Forward

I felt an urgency to bring her forward, to help her reach the place of union with her groom. But she remained rooted, as though waiting for something beyond my understanding.

Let your waist be girded and your lamps burning; And you yourselves be like men who wait for their lord. (Luke 12:35-36, NKJV).

This scripture reminds us that the church must be "girded" or prepared, not waiting passively in the background but actively anticipating her Bridegroom.

Prayer

Heavenly Father,
Lord, cleanse Your bride, that we may be without spot or wrinkle, holy and blameless in Your sight. Teach us to walk in purity and righteousness, longing for Your presence, our lamps filled with oil of Your Spirit. Help us remain in constant prayer, building one another up in faith and love as we await the day of Christ's return. In Jesus Mighty Name we pray. Amen.

Spiritual Preparation and Holiness

Her white gown symbolized purity, and she looked prepared, yet she wasn't stepping into the place where she belonged.

Therefore, having these promises, beloved, let us cleanse ourselves from all filthiness of the flesh and spirit, perfecting holiness in the fear of God. (2 Corinthians 7:1, NKJV.

19

The bride's purity and readiness reflect the call for the church to live in holiness, a state of spiritual preparation. But the dream warns that even with outward purity, true readiness requires standing in the right place, anticipating His arrival.

(1 Thessalonians 4:7 NKJV), says, For God did not call us to uncleanness, but in holiness.

Prayer

My Lord, I pray that you give me a pure heart, as I am jaded by the hurts of this world. Correct me when I go astray and bring me back to You, my Eternal Father. Amen.

A Bride in Waiting

She stood patiently, gazing out the window, waiting. I realized the church is waiting in many ways, yet she must also prepare actively for the Lord

You also be patient. Establish your hearts, for the coming is at hand. (James 5:8, NKJV).

This verse calls the church to stand firm, not as a passive bystander but as one actively preparing, knowing the bridegroom's return is near.

(Psalm 37:7 NKJV), Says, "Rest in the Lord and wait patiently for Him; Do not fret because of him who prospers in his way.

The Invitation to Be Ready

The dream left me with an impression of unfinished preparation. It was a call, an invitation for the church to come forward, to take her place at the altar, ready for her union with Christ.

Many people think religion offers nothing but Judgment. But Jesus came not to condemn but to save. His purpose was to offer life to dying humanity, inviting us to experience forgiveness, healing, and hope. The same Jesus who issues this invitation wields the power to withdraw it from those who refuse His call and continue their habits of rebellion and sin **(Rev.22:14, 15, 18, 19)**. Just as He has Authority not to welcome us. Still, He graciously choose to offer life to sinful people.

And the Spirit and the bride says, 'Come!' And let him who hears say, 'Come! (Revelation 22:17, NKJV).

This concluding verse of the Bible echoes the invitation. The church, the bride, must not only prepare but also actively call out, "Come!"—a longing for the return of Christ, her true Bridegroom.

Whatever confusion you might feel about religion, don't miss God's gracious offer, Jesus wants to forgive your sins and welcome you into new life. If you haven't already accepted His invitation, do it now. Choose this moment to begin the journey that leads to eternal life.

Prayer

Heavenly Father, I come to you in humility and repentance. I acknowledge that I am a sinner and have fallen short of Your glory. I believe that Jesus Christ is Your son, who died for my sins and rose again to give me eternal life. Lord Jesus, I invite You into my heart. Make me new. I surrender my life to you and ask You to guide me by Your Holy Spirit. Thank You for Your mercy, grace, and love. From this day forward, I will follow You and live for Your glory.

(Revelation 2:7 NKJV), says, He who has an ear, let him hear what the Spirit says to the churches. To him who overcomes I will give to eat from the tree of life, which is in the midst of the Paradise of God.

The church should be a beacon of hope, a sanctuary where light dispels the darkness. But in these last days, there is an urgency to understand how deception can infiltrate even the sacred. This dream begins with a revelation I received through a vivid dream—a prophetic vision warning of a spiritual darkness pervading the church. It is a call to vigilance, discernment, and awakening, echoing biblical truths that remain relevant in today's world.

Chapter 3

The Dream: Demons In the Church

Dream Date: April 16, 2024

In my dream, I found myself in a church. It was packed with people, but the setting was unsettlingly dark. I held a small, white candle in my hand. The candle was melting, and its light was faint, barely illuminating the space around me. As I looked around, I could sense something was wrong. The atmosphere was heavy, oppressive, and void of peace. In that moment, I wondered, why is it so dark in here?

A Revelation of Darkness

I held the candle higher, hoping to see beyond the shadows. But instead of seeing familiar faces, I saw creatures—demons lurking among the people. Even the preacher, standing tall in the pulpit, had transformed into a towering, demonic figure. I was struck by the horrifying reality that the very people who should be shepherds and protectors of the flock were themselves enshrouded in darkness

Prophetic Insight – Spiritual Darkness in High Places

This dream was not just a figment of the imagination. It held a warning—one deeply rooted in the Word of God. As the Apostle Paul warns in **(2 Corinthians 11:14-15)**, "...for Satan himself masquerades as an angel of light. It is not surprising, then, if his servants also masquerade as servants of righteousness. Even in our churches, there can be deceivers in positions of influence. They may appear holy, but their true nature is hidden under a facade of light.

The Lamp of the Body

My candle, barely flickering, held prophetic significance. **(Matthew 6:22-23)** tells us, "The eye is the lamp of the body. If your eyes are healthy, your whole body will be full of light. But if your eyes are unhealthy, your whole body will be full of darkness." In my dream, the light within the church was dim, suggesting that the spiritual vision of those inside was clouded. Perhaps they had unknowingly accepted darkness, allowing their discernment to fade.

Insight – The Spirit of Deception

The prophet Isaiah warned of such a time: **(Isaiah 5:20)** states, "Woe to those who call evil good and good evil, who put darkness for light and light for darkness..." This scripture directly speaks to the deception within the church today, where compromise can lead to confusion and, ultimately, to darkness. Without the unwavering light of Christ, even believers may find themselves led astray by teachings that distort the truth.

A Choice to Escape

In my dream, I realized I had to leave. I noticed a door slightly ajar, with brightness beyond it. This door was a beacon of hope—a pathway to freedom from the darkness. In **(John 10:9)**, Jesus speaks of Himself as the Door, saying, "I am the door; whoever enters through me will be saved." This escape was not an abandonment of faith, but a call to step out of deception and into the true light of Christ.

Boldness to Speak the Truth

Before I left, I turned and declared, "I'm going to get a friend and come back." This was not just a clever excuse to leave but a proclamation—a desire to return with truth and help others find their way out. (Ephesians 5:11) urges believers, "Have nothing to do with the fruitless deeds of darkness, but rather expose them." Speaking out against deception is not easy, yet we are called to be bold and to bring light into dark places.

The Grip of Darkness

As I reached for the door, a dark figure—one of the demons—grabbed my arm, attempting to pull me back. Yet it was unable to hold me. In (James 4:7), we are encouraged, "Submit yourselves to God. Resist the devil, and he will flee from you." This grip symbolized the attempts of the enemy to keep us bound in deception. But those who cling to Christ will be empowered to escape, no matter how dark the place.

The Call to Repentance

This dream is a call to repentance, both personally and within the church. As it says in (Revelation 3:17-18), the Lord warns of a church that sees itself as rich yet is "wretched, pitiful, poor, blind, and naked." My dream revealed a church filled with people content in the darkness. To walk in true light, we must open our eyes, allow Christ to reveal any darkness within us, and turn wholeheartedly toward Him.

The Bible uses prophetic scripture to describe the rise of corrupt and oppressive systems, or "industries," that stray from God's intent. For example, **(Revelation 18:2-3)** speaks of the fall of Babylon as a symbol of a corrupt society: "Fallen! Fallen is Babylon the Great! She has become a dwelling for demons and a haunt for every impure spirit... For all the nations have drunk the maddening wine of her adulteries." This scripture conveys the way earthly systems can become spiritual "industries" of deception, leading people astray through greed, falsehood, and idolatry. Similarly, **(Micah 2:1-2)** warns against those who scheme in darkness for personal gain, exploiting others for wealth or power. These passages highlight a prophetic message about the dangers of worldly systems when they prioritize profit or influence over truth and justice, a reminder of the need for discernment and integrity within both the church and society.

Surely the Lord GOD does nothing. Unless He reveals His secret counsel to His servants the prophets. (Amos 3:7, NKJV).

Dreams and visions have long served as a bridge between the physical and spiritual realms, offering glimpses of what God reveals to us as His people. This book is a testament to the power of these revelations, given not to predict or control but to warn, guide, and prepare. Through these dreams, God has provided a window into the state of our world and a call for vigilance and repentance. As you journey through these pages, may you find light, wisdom, and understanding in His Word, which is our foundation and guide.

Purpose of Prophetic Dreams

And it shall come to pass afterward, that I will pour out My Spirit on all flesh; Your sons and your daughters shall prophesy, Your old men shall dream dreams, your young men shall see visions. (Joel 2:28, NKJV).

Prophetic dreams are God's way of speaking to us, often hidden in symbols and signs, waiting for interpretation. Throughout the Bible, God has used dreams to communicate vital messages, to warn, and to lead His people. Joel 2:28 reminds us that we are living in times when the Spirit of God continues to pour out upon us. Dreams are given for a purpose, and when we listen, these divine messages can inspire, guide, and correct us, aligning us with God's will.

Chapter 4

Dream of the White House and the Sealed Door

Dream Date: October 28, 2024

The key to the house of David; I will lay on his shoulder; so he shall open, and no one shall shut; And he shall shut, and no one shall open, (Isaiah 22:22 NKJV).

On October 28, 2024, I received a dream in the days leading up to the election. In this dream, it was a bright day, and the White House stood in front of me, majestic and powerful. As I walked up the steps, I noticed the door was open, inviting me in. But just as I placed my foot on the first step, the door shut, sealing tightly with a unique handle—a handle that resembled a jigsaw puzzle, with the United States and the presidential seal interlocked. The door was sealed so tightly that no one could open it.

Isaiah 22:22 captures the essence of this vision: that some doors God alone can open and shut. The image of a tightly sealed White House hints at a divine control over the nation's leadership and the times to come, reminding us that while earthly power may seem accessible, God remains the ultimate authority.

Symbolism of the Sealed Door

The king's heart is in the hands of the Lord; like rivers of water; He turns it wherever He wishes (Proverbs 21:1, NKJV).

This dream speaks to the sovereignty of God over nations and leaders. The jigsaw puzzle handle suggests a complex and tightly held authority, one that no human effort can access without divine permission. In **(Proverbs 21:1)**, we are reminded that God alone directs the course of rulers and nations. The sealed door serves as a symbol that ultimate power rests with God, not man. It encourages us to trust that He holds the keys, guiding the course of events according to His will.

Let's reflect on the powerful prophetic dreams I shared so far. They speak deeply to spiritual discernment, biblical preparation. Here's a brief reflection on each core theme.

Dream of the Bride and the Church

Let us rejoice and be glad and give him glory! For the wedding of the Lamb has come, and his bride has made herself ready. (Revelation 19:7).

This dream revealed the image of a church where a bride, dressed in beautiful white, was waiting. The church was bright, yet empty, and the bride stood alone, looking out of a window. When I asked her about her bridegroom, she responded, "I don't have one," which left me puzzled. It became clear that this bride was not waiting for a human groom but for the Lord Jesus Christ. (Revelation 19:7) speaks of the Bride of Christ the

Church—making herself ready for His return. This vision calls the Church to awaken, to prepare, and to wait with hope and purity for the return of her true Bridegroom.

The Bride's Readiness

Behold, I am coming soon, bringing my recompense with me, to repay each one for what he has done. (Revelation 22:12).

The image of the bride waiting serves as a powerful reminder of the Church's role in these times. Revelation 22:12 reminds us of Christ's promise to return. The bride's gaze out the window symbolizes a longing, a readiness for the Lord's coming. Yet her position at the back of the church speaks to a need for the Church to bring herself forward, to be visible and ready. This vision challenges us to examine our own readiness and commitment, calling us to live as those truly expecting the Lord's return.

Dream of Demons in the Church

For such men are false apostles, deceitful workmen, disguising themselves as apostles of Christ. And no wonder, for Satan himself masquerades as an angel of light. (2 Corinthians 11:13-14).

In a haunting dream, I found myself in a dark, crowded church holding a melting candle. As I raised the candle, I saw that the church was filled with demons, including a tall figure standing at the pulpit. I saw a slightly cracked door leading to the outside light, and I knew I needed to leave. This vision exposed the presence of deception within places of worship. (2 **Corinthians 11:13-14**) warns us of false teachers, reminding us that even Satan masquerades as an angel of light. This dream calls for spiritual discernment, urging us to remain faithful to the true light of Christ.

The Light of the Candle

Your word is a lamp to my feet and a light to my path. (Psalm 119:105).

The candle in my hand symbolized the Word of God, a light in the darkness, illuminating truth amidst deception. As the candle melted, it revealed the hidden darkness around me. This dream emphasizes the necessity of God's Word as our guide, shining truth into every shadow. **(Psalm 119:105)** reminds us that His Word is the only true light, leading us on a path of righteousness and helping us recognize and avoid falsehood.

Reflection on the Need for Discernment

Beloved do not believe every spirit, but test the spirits to see whether they are from God, because many false prophets have gone out into the world. (1 John 4:1).

The dream challenges us to test the spirits, discerning truth from lies. In a time when deception is prevalent, we are called to guard ourselves with the truth of God's Word. **(1 John 4:1)** urges us to test all things, keeping only what is true and holy. This vision serves as a warning, urging the Church to remain vigilant and to hold fast to the Word of God as our anchor.

Summary and Call to Reflection

For nothing is hidden that will not be made manifest, nor is anything secret that will not be known and come to light." (Luke 8:17).

These opening dreams provide a foundation for what is to come, revealing truths about the state of our world, the Church, and the times we are living in **(Luke 8:17)** assures us that all hidden things will be brought to light. As we proceed, let us be mindful of these revelations, using them as a call to draw closer to God, to deepen our understanding, and to stand firm in His truth.

Prayers

These closing prayers are reflections on the visions and dreams shared in the first 4 chapters of this book. They call for remembrance, repentance, and renewed focus on God. Each dream serves as a warning, a reminder, and a guide, urging us to turn to God wholeheartedly and prepare ourselves spiritually.

Prayers of Recall

Prayer for Spiritual Memory
Lord, help us recall the visions You reveal to us. Give us spiritual memory, so we don't forget the warnings You've sent. As in the dream of the concentration camp, You reminded us of the cost of unrepentance and the need for protection. We ask that You bring these visions to our minds when we need them most, prompting us to act with wisdom and faith.

Prayer for clarity of Revelation

Father, grant us the clarity to understand the meanings of Your revelations. Like the young man in the dream, help us see beyond what is seen, to discern what You are truly saying through each vision. Clear our minds of worldly confusion so we can clearly hear Your voice.

Personal Repentance Prayer

Lord, forgive us for our sins. Show us where we have gone astray, whether through actions, thoughts, or inaction. In the dream of the bride, waiting and unclaimed, You revealed that we are not ready. Help us to repent deeply, turning from sin with true sorrow, so we can be the pure bride You desire.

Repentance for the Nation

Lord, we lift up our nation to You. Just as the White House dream showed a closed door with no way in, we recognize that our nation's path is unclear. Bring repentance to our land so that we may find our way back to You, reopening the door for Your guidance and presence.

Prayer to See with Godly Vision

God, help us keep our eyes fixed on You, even in dark times. Just as the demons filled the church in the dream, we know that the world can be filled with distractions, fears, and forces against us. Let us lift our eyes toward You, the Light, so we may walk in Your truth without wavering.

Prayer for Strength in Trials

Lord, grant us strength to remain steadfast. When challenges arise, let our focus on You be unshakable. Give us the faith to hold our candle high, no matter how small the light may seem in a world of darkness. Help us to press forward with unwavering faith.

Prayer of Dedication and Commitment

Heavenly Father, as we conclude this journey, we dedicate our lives anew to Your service. May the dreams and revelations shared here deepen our walk with You. Empower us to be vigilant, compassionate, and courageous in proclaiming Your truth. Keep our hearts attentive to Your voice, always ready to heed Your call.

Final Reflection

Let each reader be encouraged to take these dreams as a call to action. Hold tightly to God's promises, walk in righteousness, and seek Him daily. May we all grow in understanding, in prayer, and in faith, becoming lights in a world that desperately needs the hope and peace that only God can provide.

Chapter 5

The Prophetic Dream of the Multitude in White

December 2024

It was a bright day, the kind that felt almost supernatural—where the light wasn't just shining but radiating with divine intensity. As I stood in an open field, I took in the beauty before me. The grass was lush and green, untouched, stretching endlessly as if prepared for something sacred.

Then, I saw them. Hundreds of people, all dressed in white, moving together in perfect unity. Their garments flowed as they walked, and each one had a white covering over their head, resembling the attire of biblical times. There was no hesitation in their steps—each one moved in sync, as though led by an unseen force, marching toward a destination unknown to me.

There was something powerful, almost holy, about the sight. Their unity was unshakable, their purpose undeniable. Though I could not hear their voices, their very presence spoke volumes. They were on a mission, moving with a divine urgency, completely surrendered to whatever calling had brought them together.

I watched in awe, my spirit stirred with a deep sense of reverence. Who were they? Where were they going? What was their purpose? Before I could grasp the full meaning, I woke up, my heart still pounding with the weight of what I had just witnessed.

A Call to the Chosen

This dream is a prophetic revelation—a call to God's people to rise up, walk in purity, and move in unity. The open field represents the vast harvest of souls **(Matthew 9:37-38)**. The bright day symbolizes the illumination of God's truth, calling His people out of darkness and into His marvelous light **(1 Peter 2:9)**.

The multitude in white represents the remnant—God's chosen people, clothed in righteousness and set apart for His divine purpose **(Revelation 19:8)**. Their synchronized movement reflects the unity of the Spirit **(Ephesians 4:3-6)**, showing that in these last days, God is raising up a people who will walk in one accord, fully aligned with His will.

This vision is not just for me but for all who are called to stand for righteousness. It is a reminder that the time is now to prepare, to move in faith, and to be part of God's great mission. The question is:

Will you answer the call?

Shadows In the Park

Dream Date: December 12, 2024

In this dream, my daughter and I were walking through an area that resembled a park. It was crowded with people, yet darkness loomed over the scene. Shadows covered the faces of individuals, and as I looked closer, I noticed something alarming: every person had a demon beside them, whispering into their ears.

As we continued walking, my spiritual sight sharpened, and I saw Satan himself in his rare form. He was speaking persistently into someone's ear, his influence evident in the person's demeanor. Without hesitation, I declared, "I see you. I break you in the mighty name of Jesus! Be gone!" At my words, the enemy recoiled, his power broken.

Moving forward, I saw demons gathering around children, whispering deceit and fear into their young minds. My heart was heavy as I realized how the enemy targets the most vulnerable, seeking to corrupt the innocence of future generations.

I awoke with a strong conviction to pray for discernment, protection, and authority over spiritual darkness. This dream reminds us of the reality of spiritual warfare and the urgent need to stand firm in Christ.

Spiritual Warfare

For though we walk in the flesh, we do not war according to the flesh, For the weapons of our warfare are not carnal but mighty in God for pulling down strongholds. **(2 Corinthians 10:3-4. NKJV).**

This dream illustrates the unseen battle raging around us and our responsibility as believers to engage in prayer and stand firm in God's truth.

Authority in Christ

Behold, I give unto you power to tread on serpents and scorpions, and over all the power of the enemy: and nothing shall by any means hurt you. **(Luke 10:19)** God has given us authority to confront and overcome spiritual darkness, as shown when Satan fled at the command of Jesus' name.

Protecting the Innocent

Train up a child in the way he should go; even when he is old, he will not depart from it. **(Proverbs 22:6)**. Children are a target for the enemy, but through prayer and teaching, we can shield them and guide them toward God's truth.

The Power of the Name of Jesus

The victory in the December 12 dream came not through my strength but through the name of Jesus. His name carries authority over every power of darkness.

Therefore, God exalted Him to the highest place and gave Him the name that is above every name, that at the name of Jesus every knee should bow, in heaven and on earth and under the earth. **(Philippians 2:9-10).**

When I spoke the name of Jesus, Satan fled. This is a reminder to every believer that we are not powerless in the face of spiritual attacks.

Pray Without Ceasing

The prayer of a righteous person is powerful and effective. **(James 5:16).**

Speak the Word of God

Jesus defeated Satan by declaring Scripture: "It is written: 'Man shall not live on bread alone. **(Matthew 4:4).**

Walk in Authority

"I have given you authority to trample on snakes and scorpions and to overcome all the power of the enemy; nothing will harm you." (Luke 10:19)

Protecting the Next Generation:

The children in the dream symbolize the enemy's target: the next generation. The whispers represent lies designed to pull them away from the truth of God.

As parents, mentors, and believers, we have a God-given responsibility to cover our children in prayer, teach them His Word, and model a life of faith.

"Fathers, do not provoke your children to anger, but bring them up in the discipline and instruction of the Lord." **(Ephesian 6:4).**

Pray Daily for Children:
"The Lord will keep you from all harm—He will watch over your life." **(Psalm 121:7).**

Teach Them God's Word:
"Fix these words of mine in your hearts and minds; tie them as symbols on your hands and bind them on your foreheads. Teach them to your children." **(Deuteronomy 11:18-19).**

Be Watchful:
Speak the Word of God, Jesus defeated Satan by declaring Scripture: It is written: 'Man shall not live on bread alone. **(Matthew 4:4).**

Prayer for the Next Generation

Heavenly Father,
In the mighty name of Jesus Christ, we come before You today
on behalf of the next generation. Lord, You are their refuge and
fortress, their God in whom they can trust **(Psalm 91:2)**. We
plead the blood of Jesus over their minds, hearts, and spirits.

Father, hide them under the shadow of Your wings and cover
them from every evil scheme of the enemy. Silence the dark
whispers that try to tell lies, fear, and deception into their ears.
Let every evil spirit that seeks to confuse, tempt, or oppress
them be bound and cast out in Jesus' name.

Lord, surround them with Your angels of protection. Guard
their paths, their friendships, their choices, and their future. Let
the voice of the Holy Spirit be louder than any shadow of
darkness. Place Your Word deep within their hearts so they will
not sin against You **(Psalm 119:11)**.

Raise in them a generation of bold believers who will not bow
to the idols of this world but will shine as lights in the midst of
darkness **(Philippians 2:15)**. Protect their innocence,
strengthen their faith, and clothe them with the full armor of
God so they may stand against the schemes of the enemy
(Ephesians 6:11).

We declare that no weapon formed against them shall prosper,
and every tongue that rises against them in judgment You will
condemn **(Isaiah 54:17)**. They belong to You, Lord Jesus, and
You have called them for such a time as this. In the mighty
name of Jesus Christ, we pray,
Amen.

The House of Old Bones

Dream Date: January 20, 2020

I found myself walking in a desolate park. The ground was covered with dirt, uneven and unsettling, with mounds that resembled freshly made graves. From these hills of dirt, strange creepy bugs crawled out, adding an air of dread to the scene. Though I walked alone, it felt as if an unseen presence accompanied me, intensifying my unease.

Ahead, I saw a peculiar gate, its structure framed by two open windows and a door that appeared slightly Ajar. Compelled by curiosity and a search for understanding, I approached and opened the gate. As I stepped closer, I noticed a woman inside—a figure from a bygone era, her head wrapped, sweeping dirt back and forth while humming an eerie tune.

I asked her, "Is this a park?"
Her response sent chills through me: "This is the house of old bones." She began naming five names I couldn't quite recall, adding, "On the shell of water, the house of old generals."

She invited me to step inside, but a deep discernment warned me to refuse. I closed the door, stepping back, but she reached out and grabbed my arm. My heart raced as I realized the danger. Freeing my hands, I placed one on her head and raised the other in prayer to God, seeking His protection.

As I prayed, her face began to shift, revealing a demonic countenance. The oppressive presence around her grew stronger, but I continued to call on the name of the Lord, unwavering in faith. Her transformation revealed the truth of evil in that place.

Suddenly, I awoke, startled by the touch of my Bible resting beside my bed. I realized that God's Word had been my shield, guarding my spirit even in the darkest of dreams.

The Valley of Dry Bones

The hand of the Lord came upon me out in the spirit of the Lord and set me down in the midst of the valley; and it was full of bones. (**Ezekiel 37:1 NKJV**).

The imagery of the "house of old bones" recalls Ezekiel's vision of dry bones, where God's power is displayed in bringing life to what was dead. This dream stands as a stark contrast, where the enemy seeks to deceive and trap.

Testing the Spirits

Beloved do not believe every spirit, but test the spirits, whether they are from God. (**1 John 4:1 NKJV**).

The woman's invitation symbolizes the devil's subtle attempts to lure us into spiritual danger. Discernment, guided by God, helps us recognize and resist such traps.

The Power of Prayer

"Therefore, submit to God. Resist the devil and he will flee from you."(**James 4:7 NKJV**). Placing my hands on her head and praying demonstrated the authority believers have in Christ. The enemy's power is nullified when we stand firm in prayer and faith.

The Word as a Weapon

Take the helmet of salvation and the sword of the Spirit, which is the word of God.

The Holy Bible affirmed that the Word of God is our spiritual weapon and shield. Even when unconscious, God's Word provides protection and guidance. Placing my hands on her head and praying demonstrated the authority.

The Gate of Decision

In the distance, a peculiar gate appeared. It was framed by two open windows and a door that looked ajar. The structure seemed misplaced, out of time and context, but it beckoned me forward. When I reached it, curiosity mixed with caution as I opened the gate to glimpse what lay beyond.

Inside, I saw a woman dressed in old-fashioned attire. Her head was wrapped, and she swept dirt back and forth in repetitive motions, humming a haunting tune. Her movements, though seemingly mundane, carried an otherworldly heaviness.

When I asked her, "Is this a park?" she stopped and turned to me, her words piercing the stillness: "This is the house of old bones."

Enter by the narrow gate; For wide is the gate and broad is the way that leads to destruction, and there are many who go in by it. Because narrow is the gate and difficult is the way which leads to life, and there are few who find it. **(Matthew 7:13-14 NKJV).**

The gate represented a choice, a moment of spiritual testing. Would I venture further into the unknown, or would I heed the unease in my spirit? God often provides such crossroads to reveal His wisdom and direction.

The Names and the Invitation

The woman continued, naming five names I could not recall upon waking. There was something cryptic about her words: "On the shell of water, the house of old generals." Her language felt like riddles meant to confuse or mislead.

Then came the invitation: "Come in," she said. Her voice, though calm, carried an undercurrent of demand. It was a moment of decision, and the Holy Spirit within me sounded an alarm. This was no ordinary place, and this woman was no ordinary figure.

I refused and stepped back, closing the door. But her reach was swift—she grabbed my arm, pulling me toward her.

Be sober, be vigilant; because your adversary the devil walks about like a roaring lion, seeking whom he may devour. Resist him, steadfast in the faith. **(1 Peter 5:8-9 NKJV)**.

The enemy often disguises his traps in the guise of curiosity or welcome, luring us into spiritual danger. This verse reinforces the need for vigilance and resistance the believers have in Christ. The enemy's power is nullified when we stand firm in prayer and faith.

The Word as a Weapon

Take the helmet of salvation and the sword of the Spirit, which is the word of God. **(Ephesians 6:17 NKJV)**.

Waking to the touch of my Bible affirmed that the Word of God is our spiritual weapon and shield. Even when unconscious, God's Word provides protection and guidance.

The Power of Prayer

With her grip tightening, I knew this was not a battle of flesh and blood. Instinctively, I raised my free hand to God in prayer, while placing my other hand on her head. As I prayed, the power of the Lord surged through me.

Her face began to change—what was once human now shifted into a demonic form. This transformation revealed her true nature, and though her appearance grew more terrifying, I held firm in prayer.

The Lord is my light and my salvation, whom shall, I fear? The Lord is the stronghold of my life—of whom shall I be afraid? (**Psalm 27:1 NIV**). When we stand in faith and call on God, the forces of darkness have no power over us. This moment affirmed that victory is not achieved through human strength but through spiritual reliance on the Almighty.

Awakening to the Word

Suddenly, I awoke. The sensation of her grip was replaced by the gentle touch of my Bible resting beside my bed. I realized then that God's Word had been my anchor, even as I faced spiritual confrontation. The holy Bible is not merely a book, it is a living, active force, sharper than any double-edged sword (**Hebrews 4:12**).

Your word is a lamp to my feet, and a light to my path. (Psalm 119:105 NKJV).

God has been revealing dreams to me in accelerated pace. I would like to introduce you to another dream that I had. The White Horse Dream one month before the COVID-19 lockdowns were put in place in America in early 2020. The Lord showed it to me ahead of time, and I immediately shared the dream on my YouTube channel, Donnalisa385. At that point, most people had no idea what was about to happen, but God had already revealed it. When the lockdowns began, I understood that the dream was a prophetic warning of what was coming.

Chapter 6

The White Horse Dream/ Revelation Dream

Dream Date: February 20, 2020

The Sound of Wings

At 5:30 a.m., I awoke from a vivid and spiritually significant dream. It began with the sound of powerful wings flying overhead, the noise so distinct and commanding that it filled the atmosphere. I looked out the window, and my attention was drawn to children gazing skyward, their faces marked by awe and curiosity.

When I lifted my eyes to the heavens, a vision unfolded. A majestic white horse with transparent wings raced powerfully across the sky. Its speed and strength were otherworldly, yet there was a purposeful elegance in movements. The horse suddenly paused, hovering mid-air, and shifted directions—right, left, and then back to the center before coming to a stop.

"Then I looked, and behold, a whirlwind was coming out of the north, a great cloud with raging fire engulfing itself (Ezekiel 1:4 NKJV).

The white horse in the dream resonates with biblical imagery of God's messengers, often associated with power, judgment, and divine purpose.

Multiplication and Movement

What happened next was extraordinary. The single white horse multiplied into many horses, each moving in a specific direction north, south, east, and west. Their movements were deliberate, as though carrying out assignments in different corners of the earth.

As I marveled at this display, I noticed a plane falling from the sky, a harbinger of destruction. The horses' wings emitted a strange energy, resembling spiritual forces that entered homes, flowing under doors like an invisible current.

And I looked, and behold, a white horse. He who sat on it had a bow; and a crown was giving to him, and he went out conquering and to conquer. (Revelation 6:2 NKJV).

The multiplication of horses symbolizes a spreading of divine action across the earth. While **(Revelation 6:2)** often refers to conquest, in the dream, the energy from the wings speaks to the spiritual impact—an awakening for some and judgment for others.

A Call to Prayer

When the children saw the plane falling and connected the events to the horse, their awe turned to fear. They ran to their homes, seeking safety from what they now realized was not merely beautiful but also a harbinger of destruction.

In this moment, I turned to my family with urgency. "We need to pray," I said, rounding everyone up. My middle son, however, seemed intent on preparing for church, looking for something to place in his Bible. I stopped him and said, "We're not going to church—we must pray."

This was not a time for ritual or routine; it was a call to seek God directly. My eldest son attempted to block the energy from entering under the door, but I knew that human efforts alone would not suffice.

Be anxious for nothing, but in everything by prayer and supplication, with thanksgiving, let your request be made known to God; and the peace of God, which surpasses all understanding, will guard your hearts and minds through Christ Jesus. (Philippians 4:6 NKJV).

The urgency to pray reflects the understanding that spiritual battle are fought and won in the presence of God.

The Family in Unity

As fear gripped the household, I gathered my family in the living room. My granddaughter clung to her father for comfort, and we all sat in a circle on the floor, holding hands. We recited the Lord's Prayer together:

"Our Father, who art in heaven, hallowed be Thy name..."

The atmosphere shifted as we unified in prayer, turning our hearts toward God. It was then that I began to plead the blood of Jesus over my family, invoking His protection against the unseen forces entering the world.

And they overcame him by the blood of the lamb and by the word of their testimony, and they did not love their lives to the death. (Revelation 12:11 NKJV).

49

The blood of Jesus is the ultimate shield against spiritual attacks, a testimony of His victory over sin and death.

Turning to the Gospel

The television, left on during the chaos, caught my attention. It displayed a random channel, but I instructed, "If you're going to leave that on, we must turn to the Gospel."

The act of turning to the Gospel reflects the need to anchor ourselves in God's Word during times of spiritual turbulence. As we concluded our prayer, huddled together in humility, the sense of fear lifted, replaced by peace and confidence in the Lord's protection.

Your word is a lamp to my feet and a light to my path. (Psalm 119:105 NKJV).

God's Word illuminates the way forward, providing comfort and direction in the midst of uncertainty.

Let the word of Christ dwell in you richly in all wisdom, teaching and admonishing one another in psalms and hymns and spiritual song, singing with grace in you hearts to the Lord. (Colossians 3:16 NKJV).

The decision to turn to the gospel reflects the necessity of anchoring ourselves in God's truth. His words dispel fear and bring peace amid chaos.

This dream is a call to spiritual vigilance, a reminder of the power of prayer, and a testament to the importance of unity in seeking God's protection. It emphasizes that while the signs of the times may be alarming, believers are called to respond not in fear but in faith, standing firm in the promises of God.

The Black Horse Dream and the Pouring of God's Spirit

Dream Date: March 13, 2020

The Sunset and the Sky

On the evening of March 13, 2020, at 4:02 a.m., I awoke from a vivid and powerful dream. It began at sunset, the sky streaked with fiery orange and deep purple hues. As I gazed upward, the number 9:48 appeared, written boldly across the sky. Behind it, I saw a black horse with a rider, racing swiftly across the horizon.

The horse moved with a fierce urgency, its hooves pounding the ground as though marking the arrival of a significant moment. Then, a voice echoed across the heavens: "I am pouring My Spirit." The sound was unmistakable, powerful, divine, and commanding. I awoke with the weight of the dream pressing upon me, deeply stirred by its meaning.

Interpretation of the Dream

The Sunset: A Closing Window of Time

The dream began at sunset, symbolizing the end of a day or an era. Biblically, the setting sun often marks a transition, a warning that time is running out.

And it shall come to pass in that day," says the Lord God, "that I will make the sun go down at noon. And I will darken the earth in broad daylight. **(Amos 8:9) NKJV.**

The sunset in this dream represents spiritual urgency. The window for repentance is closing, and God is calling His people to awaken and prepare.

Number 9:48: A Divine Message

The number 9:48 stood boldly in the sky, a symbol that demands attention. When broken down, the numbers carry significant biblical meaning:

Nine signifies divine completeness and finality, often marking the conclusion of God's work (e.g., Jesus' death in the ninth hour).

Forty-eight points to leadership and servanthood, as the Levites—God's chosen priests—were allotted 48 cities in the Promised Land **(Numbers 35:7)**.

Together, 9:48 is a prophetic marker: a time of divine completion and a call for leaders to rise and serve. The urgency of this number reminds us that the time for God's judgment is near, but His Spirit will guide those who answer His call.

The Black Horse and Its Rider: Judgment and Famine

The black horse is a striking symbol, directly linked to **(Revelation 6:5-6: NKJV)**.

When He opened the third seal, I heard the third living creature say, 'Come and see.' So, I looked, and behold, a black horse, and he who sat on it had a pair of scales in his hand. And I heard a voice in the midst of the four living creatures saying, 'A quart of wheat for a denarius, and three quarts of barley for a denarius; and do not harm the oil and the wine.

This horse represents famine, scarcity, and economic hardship, warning of trials to come. In the dream, the rider moved with urgency, symbolizing that these events are approaching swiftly. The scales in Revelation symbolize justice and measurement, reminding us that God's judgment will weigh the deeds of humane.

The Voice of God: The Pouring of His Spirit

The declaration, "I am pouring My Spirit," is both a warning and a promise. It reflects **(Joel 2:28-29: NKJV)**.

And it shall come to pass afterwards that I will pour out My Spirit on all flesh; Your sons and daughters shall prophesy, your old men shall dream dreams, your young men shall see visions. And also, on My menservants and on My maidservants. I will pour out My Spirit in those days.

Even amid judgment, God promises to equip His people with spiritual gifts, revelation, and guidance. This pouring of His Spirit is both a preparation for what is to come and a call to action for believers to lead others toward repentance and faith.

A Call to Action

This dream is a warning and a call for all who hear it:

Repent and Seek God's Face: The sunset signifies a closing window. Now is the time to repent and turn back to God.

Rise as Leaders and Intercessors: The number 48 calls believers to step into their roles as spiritual leaders, intercessors, and servants of God.

Prepare for Trials: The black horse signals coming challenges, but God's Spirit provides the strength and discernment to endure.

But the Lord is faithful, who will establish you and guard you from the evil one. **(2 Thessalonians 3:3).**

Prayers for Preparation
As we reflect on this dream, let us pray for guidance, strength, and spiritual readiness:

Prayer of Repentance

Heavenly Father, we humble ourselves before You, repenting of our sins. Forgive us and cleanse us by the blood of Jesus. Turn our hearts back to You and help us to walk in Your ways.

Prayer for Leadership:
Lord, raise up leaders in this time of urgency. Empower us with Your Spirit to guide others, speak the truth, and intercede for our families and communities.

Prayer for Strength in Trials:
Almighty God, we trust in Your faithfulness. Strengthen us to endure the trials ahead and let Your Spirit guide us through every storm. In Jesus' name, Amen.

This dream reveals both warning and hope. While the black horse signals hardship, the voice of God assures us of His presence and power. Trust in His Spirit and keep your eyes on Jesus. He is our strength, our guide, and our refuge in times of trouble.

"The name of the Lord is a strong tower; the righteous run to it and are safe." **(Proverbs 18:10) NKJV.**

Joel's Prophecy and the Black Horse Dream: A Parallel Vision

In **(Joel 2:1-2),** the prophet declares:
"Blow the trumpet in Zion; sound the alarm on my holy hill. Let all who live in the land tremble, for the day of the Lord is coming. It is close at hand, a day of darkness and gloom, a day of clouds and blackness. Like dawn spreading across the

55

mountains, a large and mighty army comes, such as never was in ancient times nor ever will be in ages to come."

This passage aligns vividly with the imagery of the black horse racing through the sky in the dream. Joel's description of a day of darkness and blackness echoes the symbolic appearance of the horse, which signifies a period of judgment and calamity. Just as Joel warns of an imminent "day of the Lord," the dream also speaks of urgency, repentance, and divine intervention.

The Call for Repentance

(Joel 2:12-13) emphasizes: "Even now," declares the Lord, return to me with all your heart, with fasting and weeping and mourning. Rend your heart and not your garments. Return to the Lord your God, for he is gracious and compassionate, slow to anger and abounding in love, and he relents from sending calamity.

In the dream, the voice declaring, "I am pouring My Spirit," signals both judgment and mercy. Joel's call to repentance mirrors the divine invitation in the dream to return to God and prepare for His outpouring of Spirit. The black horse symbolizes the urgency of this repentance before it's too late.

The Spirit's Outpouring and Hope for Renewal

(Joel 2:28-29) proclaims: And afterward, I will pour out my Spirit on all people. Your sons and daughters will prophesy, your old men will dream dreams, your young men will see visions. Even on my servants, both men and women, I will pour out my Spirit in those days."

This promise of the Spirit's outpouring directly connects to the declaration in the dream. The black horse serves as a harbinger of divine intervention, much like Joel's prophecy. While it carries a warning of judgment, it also points to the ultimate hope of restoration and renewal through the Spirit.

Joel's Warning and the Dream's Message

The dream and Joel's vision work together to emphasize:

Judgment: The black horse, like the locust army in Joel, represents the consequences of humanity's sin and a call to face divine justice.

Repentance: Both call for genuine heart transformation, urging people to return to God.

Hope: The outpouring of God's Spirit in both visions promises salvation and renewal for those who heed the warning. By weaving Joel's prophetic themes into the dream, it becomes clear that God is speaking through both visions, calling us to recognize His authority, seek His mercy, and prepare for His presence. The black horse dream is not just a warning, it reflects Joel's timeless prophecy, urging us to respond with repentance and faith.

Chapter7

The Fiery Call Dream Revelation

Dream Date: May 6, 2020

May 6, 2020 – 12:00 a.m. As I drifted into sleep, a vivid and unsettling dream unfolded. I found myself inside a house I had never seen before, babysitting two children. One was a boy, aged 12, and the other a little girl, aged 6. These children were not my own, nor were they, my grandchildren. Something about caring for them felt unusual, as I rarely babysit children outside my family.

The house had a living room shrouded in darkness, while the kitchen was brightly lit. The contrast between the two rooms was striking darkness on one side and light on the other. The children said they were hungry, so I went into the kitchen to prepare food for them.

In the kitchen, there was a sliding glass door with blinds slightly open. As I approached the door, my attention was drawn to the sky outside. Suddenly, I saw a massive ball of fire falling from the heavens. It struck the ground with a deafening boom. Moments later, another fiery ball descended, crashing to the earth with an even greater force.

Then, something extraordinary happened. I saw stars being plucked from the sky one by one, as if an invisible hand was removing them. The stars fell to the earth, their light extinguished as they touched the ground. Following this, an asteroid came hurtling down, slamming into the earth with another resounding boom.

As I stood frozen, witnessing these apocalyptic events, an angel appeared. The angel was radiant, almost translucent, yet it had a human form. Its wings were enormous, and as they flapped, the events outside seemed to accelerate. Balls of fire, asteroids, and stars fell faster and faster, as though the angel's presence intensified the chaos.

Then, fire began to seep under the door of the house. These were not ordinary flames but tiny particles of fire that rose to eye level. I heard a voice speak a single word, "Come." The voice was authoritative and reverberated throughout the atmosphere, carrying both urgency and invitation.

I heard a knock on the door and assumed it must be the children's parents. I rushed to open it, asking them, "Did you see it? Did you hear it?" They seemed unfazed, as though they had come from a casual gathering. The father held a party cup in his hand, and they walked past me into the house.
I led them to the sliding door, trying to show them what was happening outside. The balls of fire, falling stars, and fiery particles continued. The voice echoed again, "Come."

The parents looked at the scene but seemed hesitant to respond. The mother hung her head in shame, visibly burdened by guilt. Then the 12-year-old boy, with great courage, turned to his mother. He gently held her face, kissed her cheek, and said, "Mother, I love you, but I'm going."

The boy stepped forward, his decision clear. The mother stood still, unable to move. I turned to the parents and asked, "What are you going to do? Are you going to go?" The father remained silent, and the mother shook her head as tears welled up in her eyes. At that moment, the dream ended, and I woke up with the word "Come" ringing in my ears.

This dream holds profound spiritual meaning, emphasizing the urgency of repentance, the reality of judgment, and the personal choice to respond to God's call.

Fiery Judgment and Falling Stars:
Falling stars and fiery destruction mirror apocalyptic imagery in scripture. The stars of heaven fell to the earth, as a fig tree drops its late figs when it is shaken by a mighty wind. (Revelation 6:13, NKJV). The heavens will vanish away like smoke; the earth will grow old like a garment. (Isaiah 51:6, NKJV).

The Angel of Acceleration:
The angel symbolizes divine intervention and the intensification of events leading to the fulfillment of prophecy.

Then I saw another angel flying in the midst of heaven, having the everlasting gospel to preach to those who dwell on the earth. (Revelation 14:6, NKJV).

The Call to Come:
The repeated word, "Come," reflects God's invitation to salvation and eternal life. The Spirit and the bride say, 'Come!' And let him who hears say, 'Come! (Revelation 22:17, NKJV).

The Boy's Faithful Response:
The 12-year-old boy's decision to go demonstrates childlike faith and obedience to God's call. Assuredly, I say to you, unless you converted and become as little children, you will by no means enter the kingdom of heaven. (Matthew 18:3, NKJV).

Parental Hesitation:
The parents' reluctance to respond highlights the weight of sin and the danger of ignoring God's call.

How shall we escape if we neglect so great salvation? (Hebrews 2:3, NKJV).

This dream calls us to reflect on our readiness for Christ's return. Will we heed the call, or will we hesitate, burdened by earthly distractions? The choice is ours.

The imagery and themes in this dream align with passages from the Holy Bible, emphasizing divine judgment, the urgency of repentance, and the choice between life and destruction.

Fiery Judgment and Falling Stars:
The fiery balls, falling stars, and asteroids symbolize God's judgment and the upheaval of creation. These echo prophetic descriptions in the Holy Bible.

The stars of heaven and their constellations will not give their light; The sun will be darkened going forth. And the moon will not cause its light to shine. (Isaiah 13:10, NKJV).

"For the heavens will vanish away like smoke. The earth will grow old like a garment. And those who dwell in it will die like manner; (Isaiah 51:6, NKJV).

The Angel's Role in Acceleration:
The angel's presence and its impact on the events suggest divine agency, consistent with the role of angels in the Holy Bible as God's messengers and executors of His will.
He shall give His angels charge over you, to keep you in all your ways. (Psalm 91:11, NKJV).

Bless the LORD, you His angels, who excel in strength, who do His word, heeding the voice of His word. (Psalm 103:20, NKJV).

The Voice Calling "Come":

The repeated call to "Come" reflects God's invitation for repentance and return to Him. This aligns with the Holy Bible's persistent theme of God calling His people back to righteousness. Come now, and let us reason together, says the LORD, though your sins are like scarlet, they shall be as white as snow. (Isaiah 1:18, NKJV). Seek the LORD while He may be found. Call upon Him while He is near. (Isaiah 55:6, NKJV).

The Boy's Faithful Response:

The boy's willingness to respond to the call highlights the Holy Bible's emphasis on faith and obedience. Even a child is known by his deeds, whether what he does is pure and right. (Proverbs 20:11, NKJV). I will say to the north, 'Give them up!' and to the south, 'Do not keep them back!' Bring my sons from afar and my daughters from the ends of the earth. (Isaiah 43:6, NKJV).

The Parents' Hesitation:

The parents' reluctance underscores the consequences of spiritual apathy, as warned in the Holy Bible.
I called and you refused. I stretched out my hand, and no one regarded. (Proverbs 1:24, NKJV). For the turning away of the simple will slay them, and the complacency of fools will destroy them. (Proverbs 1:32, NKJV).

Call to Action:

This dream serves as a reminder that God is calling His people to make a decision. Will we respond to His invitation, or will we remain bound by our distractions and sins? The Holy Bible is rich with examples of God's mercy and warnings, urging us to choose life over destruction.

The War Cry: A Prophetic Call to Intercede for Israel

Dream Date: June 7, 2020

On June 7, 2020, at 6:00 a.m., God revealed to me a dream that would resonate with profound urgency in the years to come. At the time, I shared this dream on my YouTube channel, donnalisa385, under the leading of the Holy Spirit. Though the significance of the dream felt clear, I could not have imagined how its fulfillment would unfold.

On October 7, 2023, Israel was attacked in a tragic and unprecedented way, leaving the nation and the world in shock. For those of us who listen for God's voice, this event was a confirmation of the spiritual warnings He has been sending. My dream was not just a vision; it was a prophetic declaration, urging believers to pray, prepare, and stay alert.

Now, in 2025, as the war continues, it is undeniable that God is speaking to His saints, reminding us of the spiritual battles unfolding before our eyes. This chapter recounts the dream as I received it, explores its connection to biblical prophecy, and reflects on its fulfillment in the current times.

The Setting of the Dream

The dream began in a place I did not recognize. It wasn't my home or even my country, yet it felt as though I was living there. Everything around me was unfamiliar, but one thing stood out: Israeli flags were scattered on the ground. The flags were white and blue, bearing the Star of David, a symbol that immediately brought my attention to Israel, the nation chosen by God.

At that moment, I knew this dream carried a weight of prophetic importance. The ground beneath the flags seemed to vibrate, as though signaling that something monumental was about to happen.

Warplanes in the Sky

As I looked at the sky, the stillness broke. Warplanes flew overhead in pairs. They were fast, moving with purpose and precision, and they flew so low that I instinctively fell to the ground to avoid being hit.

The planes raced toward a military base, their trajectory clear and undeniable. Their presence filled the atmosphere with tension, a foreboding sense that something monumental was unfolding.

Warning My Mother

I turned to my mother, who was beside me, and said, "Those are warplanes."

Her response was calm, dismissive even. "No," she said. "They're just heading to the military base." But something in my spirit told me otherwise. This was not a routine movement of planes. This was a declaration, an act of preparation for something far greater. I insisted, "No, we are at war."

The Proclamation of War

Suddenly, I heard knocking. It came from all directions, urgent and loud. People were going from door to door, shouting, "We are at war! We are at war!" Their cries echoed through the air, amplifying the sense of urgency I already felt.

I repeated their words to my mother, "We are at war." But still, she resisted the reality of what was happening, insisting, "No, they're just heading to the military base."

My heart grew heavier as I realized she could not see what I saw. I turned to her again and said firmly, "No, we are at war."

A Prophetic Connection Fulfilled

When I first shared this dream on June 7, 2020, on my YouTube channel, Donnalisa385, I knew it was a warning but did not fully grasp its magnitude. Fast forward to October 7, 2023—a day that will forever be etched in history—Israel was attacked, and the world watched in shock. This event was not only a fulfillment of the warnings given in my dream but also a reminder of the prophetic significance of Israel. **(Zechariah 12:2-3)** says, "I am going to make Jerusalem a cup that sends all the surrounding peoples reeling. Judah will be besieged as well as Jerusalem. On that day, when all the nations of the earth are gathered against her, I will make Jerusalem an immovable rock for all nations This dream was not just a vision but a call to alert God's people of the times we are living in. It stands as a confirmation that God speaks to His saints, urging us to watch, pray, and intercede for His plans to unfold according to His will.

Chapter 8

The Dream of the Invasion and the Hidden Covering

Date: December 22, 2015

On December 22, 2015, I had a prophetic dream that stirred my soul and opened my spiritual eyes to a deeper level of divine protection and spiritual warfare.

In the dream, I was standing outside my grandmother's house, between her home and our next-door neighbor's. Suddenly, an invasion began. Soldiers, dressed entirely in black with only their eyes visible, appeared. They held weapons and moved with authority, forcefully entering homes. It was as if a military operation had overtaken our neighborhood.

From the skies above, helicopters hovered, and soldiers descended, jumping down and rushing into houses. Fear gripped my heart—not for myself, but for my children, who were inside sleeping. I was outside, vulnerable. I dropped low to the ground between the houses, crying out to God for help. I prayed earnestly.

Then, something miraculous happened. The soldiers walked right by me as if they could not see me. I felt covered—as though heaven had placed a veil over me. I was invisible to the invaders. Once they passed, I ran into the house, woke up my daughter, and gathered my children.

I woke up from the dream with the deep sense that God had shown me something powerful, not just for me—but for the Body of Christ.

The Intercessor – A Mother's Heart

Even in the dream, my first thought was not of myself—but my children. This reflects the intercessory role God has placed on many mothers and spiritual guardians.

(Proverbs 31:27) She looked well to the ways of her household, and eateth not the bread of idleness."

Prayer is not passive. Prayer moves heaven. My cry to God became a shield that allowed me to rescue my children. Intercessors are those who stand in the gap **(Ezekiel 22:30)**, and mothers have a powerful role in doing so for their homes.

(Isaiah 54:13) And all thy children shall be taught of the Lord; and great shall be the peace of thy children.

(Psalm 34:7) The angel of the Lord encamped round about them that fear Him, and delivered them."

The Wake-Up Call – Prepare the House

This dream is a warning, a wake-up call to the Church and families. The invasion symbolizes what is to come or what is already here spiritually—forces attempting to break into the peace of God's people. **(Joel 2:1)** Blow ye the trumpet in Zion and sound an alarm in my holy mountain.

God is calling us to be alert, cover our households in prayer, and take our positions as watchmen. The times are urgent. The enemy moves swiftly, but God's protection is swifter.

We must live in the secret place, teach our children, walk in obedience, and trust in the Lord. Just as He shielded me in the dream, He promises to be our fortress.

The Spiritual Meaning of the Soldiers

In the dream, the soldiers dressed in black with only their eyes visible represent spiritual agents of darkness, either demonic spirits or earthly forces under demonic influence. Their hidden faces symbolize deception, secrecy, and control.

(2 Corinthians 11:14-15) And no marvel; for Satan himself is transformed into an angel of light. Therefore, it is no great thing if his ministers also be transformed.

The black clothing in dreams often represents spiritual blindness, sin, or hidden evil. These soldiers weren't just invading homes—they were strategically targeting places of peace and rest.

They were disciplined, organized, and had authority, reflecting how evil operates in ranks and structure—just as the kingdom of heaven does.

(Ephesians 6:12) says, against the rulers of the darkness of this world. This reminds us that the enemy studies households, routines, and vulnerabilities. But the power of Christ breaks every assignment.

The Helicopters – Assault from Above

The dream also involved helicopters, and soldiers were jumping down into people's homes. Spiritually, helicopters represent speed, elevation, and control from the air.

In warfare, helicopters provide surveillance and air assault. Spiritually, this represents attacks that come from unexpected places, sometimes spiritual, sometimes governmental, sometimes systemic.

(Revelation 12:12) Woe to the inhabitants of the earth and of the sea! for the devil comes down unto you, having great wrath.

In the end times, Satan intensifies his warfare. But even when attacks come from above, God's covering comes from even higher.

(Psalm 121:1-2) I will lift up mine eyes unto the hills, from whence cometh my help. My help cometh from the Lord.

God sees from a higher perspective. No surprise attack can bypass His angels or His hand.

Praying Without Fear

One of the most important aspects of this dream was prayer under pressure. I didn't have time to go inside. I couldn't physically run. All I could do was pray.

(Philippians 4:6-7) Be careful for nothing; but in everything by prayer and supplication with thanksgiving let your requests be made known unto God.

(Psalm 34:17) The righteous cry, and the Lord heareth, and delivered them out of all their troubles.

This dream teaches us that prayer is not our last resort to our first response. We must train our hearts to seek God even when chaos is around us. God responds to faith—even silent, desperate faith.

God's Covering Over Families:
When I ran back into the house to gather my children, I believe God was revealing His heart for family preservation and spiritual leadership. The Lord gives a specific order in times of danger: protect the house, gather the children, and prepare for what's ahead.

(Exodus 12:3-7) (The Passover) – God commanded families to place the blood on the doorposts so the destroyer would pass by.

(Joshua 24:15) As for me and my house, we will serve the Lord.

Even in spiritual invasion, the family is God's design for strength, instruction, and preservation. The enemy attacks families for this very reason. But when we respond with prayer, unity, and repentance, the blood of Jesus becomes our shield.

Protection and Covering in Spiritual Warfare: Spiritual warfare is real, and as believers we are called to stand in the gap for our families. Covering them means praying, declaring, and standing on God's Word daily.

Cover Your Family in Prayer: He who dwells in the secret place of the Most High shall abide under the shadow of the Almighty **(Psalm 91:1, NKJV).** Pray Psalm 91 over your loved ones, declaring that they live under God's shadow and protection.

Put on the Armor of God: "Put on the whole armor of God, that you may be able to stand against the wiles of the devil **(Ephesians 6:11, NKJV)**.

Ask God to clothe you and your household with truth, righteousness, peace, faith, salvation, and His Word.

Expose the Enemy's Plans
"For nothing is secret that will not be revealed, nor anything hidden that will not be known and come to light" (**Luke 8:17, NKJV**). Pray that every hidden trap or deception against your family will be uncovered and destroyed.

Fight with Spiritual Weapons
For the weapons of our warfare are not carnal but mighty in God for pulling down strongholds (**2 Corinthians 10:4, NKJV**). Use prayer, worship, and God's Word to break strongholds and silence the lies of the enemy.

A Prayer for Divine Protection

Heavenly Father, In the name of Jesus, I thank You for Your shield of protection. Just as You hid me from the eyes of the invading soldiers in the dream, I believe You are still the God who hides His people under the shadow of His wings. Cover my home, my family, and all who trust in You.

Your Word says in (**Psalm 91:7**) A thousand shall fall at thy side, and ten thousand at thy right hand; but it shall not come nigh thee."

I declare that no evil shall befall me, nor shall any plague come near my dwelling. I plead the blood of Jesus over every doorpost of my house, and I invite Your presence to dwell here. In Jesus' name, Amen.

A Prayer for Children and Family Preservation
Lord Jesus, Just as I saw my children inside the house in the dream, I lift up every child, every son and daughter, to You. I

ask for supernatural protection, guidance, and wisdom for parents, that we may lead our children in truth. Let us not be asleep while the enemy surrounds us. Let us be awakened, discerning, and alert. Teach us how to anoint our homes with prayer and fill our hearts with faith. **(Isaiah 54:13)** says, and all thy children shall be taught of the Lord; and great shall be the peace of thy children. I declare peace over our household. No weapon formed against our legacy will prosper. Keep our children safe, sanctified, and set apart for Your glory. Amen.

A Call to Repentance

In these last days, spiritual invasions are no longer just dreams. They are warnings of what is and what is to come. God is calling His people to return to Him, tear down idols, and seek holiness. **(2 Chronicles 7:14)** If my people, which are called by my name, shall humble themselves, and pray... then will I hear from heaven, and will forgive their sin, and will heal their land.

This is a call to examine your life, your household, your habits. Is the presence of God welcomed in your home? Or has it been pushed out by compromise?

The time to repent is now. The covering of God is for the obedient, the humble, the seekers of truth.

Lord, we repent.
Forgive us for ignoring the signs, for walking in fear instead of faith. We return to You. Wash us. Cleanse our hearts. Restore our homes. Make us ready for the days ahead.

A Prayer for Spiritual Sight and Boldness
Father God, give us eyes to see what others cannot. Let us not be blind to the Spirit. Help us discern the times and recognize the tactics of the enemy.

Like Elisha prayed in (**2 Kings 6:17**) Lord, open his eyes, that he may see. Let our spiritual eyes be opened. Let us walk in boldness and not in fear. Help us stand firm in the face of warfare. When others run, let us remain in faith. When others hide, let us shine. Fill us with wisdom. Let the Word be our sword, and prayer be our weapon. In Jesus' name, Amen.

A Prayer for the Church and the Bride to Awake

Holy Spirit, Awaken the Bride of Christ. Let the Church no longer sleep. Stir up the hearts of pastors, prophets, teachers, and every believer to prepare for the hour of testing. Let us put on the armor of God. Let us walk in holiness and righteousness. Let us love one another and fight for each other in prayer. As in the dream, many houses were entered, but one was covered—may our churches and homes be covered because You dwell in them. We are not afraid. We are not forsaken. We are not alone. (**Romans 13:11**) It is high time to awake out of sleep: for now is our salvation nearer than when we believed. Lord, make us ready. Make us faithful. Make us bold. In Jesus' name, Amen.

The Dream as a Prophetic Warning

The dream of December 22, 2015, was not a nightmare, but it was a prophetic revelation. It showed a time when dark forces would move through communities, invading homes, and bringing fear. But it also revealed the supernatural power of God's covering for those who trust Him.

Just like the children of Israel during the Passover, the blood on the doorposts marked those who belonged to God.

(**Exodus 12:23**) The LORD will pass over the door and will not suffer the destroyer to come in unto your houses to smite you."

In the dream, I was hiding, though they walked right by me, they could not see me. That is the anointing of divine invisibility, reserved for God's remnant people.

Preparing the Spiritual House

Many today focus on preparing physically storing food, supplies, and defense. While there is wisdom in preparation, the most urgent preparation is spiritual.

Ask yourself

Have I cleansed my house of spiritual defilement?

Do I pray over my home and family daily?

Is my heart right with God?

(**Proverbs 24:3–4**) Through wisdom is an house builded; and by understanding it is established: And by knowledge shall the chambers be filled with all precious and pleasant riches. A house filled with prayer, worship, and obedience becomes a sanctuary, even during chaos. Let your house be a spiritual refuge.

Warning to the Church—Be Not Asleep

The invasion dream is also a warning to the Church. Many congregations are asleep, unaware of the darkness creeping in. (**Matthew 13:25**) But while men slept, his enemy came and sowed tares among the wheat. The enemy waits for slumber. But now is the time to wake up, to cry out, and to equip the saints. This is not a season of comfort, this is a season of war. Let the Church rise in intercession, fasting, and purity. Let our altars be restored and our lamps be lit.

Encouragement to Stand in the Evil Day

Even when fear tries to overtake us, remember—God is with us. **(Ephesians 6:13)** "Wherefore take unto you the whole amour of God... and having done all, to stand". In the dream, when I stood back up to run into the house, there was boldness in that moment. That is the kind of boldness God is releasing to His people today.

Stand when fear says hide.
Pray when panic says run.
Believe when darkness says it's over.

You are covered. You are chosen. You are not forgotten.

Prophetic Encouragement—You Are Hidden in Christ

Lastly, remember this truth:**(Colossians 3:3)** For ye are dead, and your life is hidden with Christ in God. You are hidden in Christ. That means no matter what is coming upon this earth— plague, war, or invasion—you are covered by the blood of Jesus. Just like the soldiers passed by me in the dream, they will pass over you. Just like my daughter was asleep inside, God will keep our children in perfect peace. Just like I found strength to rise and run. God will give us courage when it's needed most. The darkness may rise, but the light inside you is greater.

Spiritual Warfare Is Real in these end times, we are not just fighting physical enemies—we are battling spiritual powers that desire to overtake families, homes, churches, and entire nation

(Ephesians 6:12) For we wrestle not against flesh and blood, but against principalities, against powers, against the rulers of the darkness of this world, against spiritual wickedness in high places."

What I saw in the dream—soldiers invading homes and helicopters swarming neighborhoods—was a reflection of the spiritual battle that is increasing around us.

We must

Guard our gates (what we watch, hear, allow in our homes).
We must guard the gates of our hearts and homes by being careful about what we watch, hear, and allow in, for these things shape our spirit and atmosphere. Protecting these gates keeps our families covered and aligned with God's truth, closing the door to the enemy's influence.

Anoint our doorposts with oil and prayer
When we anoint our doorposts with oil and prayer, we are setting a boundary of protection, declaring that our homes belong to the Lord. This act is a symbol of covering, inviting God's presence while driving away the enemy's influence
.

Declare war in the spirit against every demonic strategy
We declare war in the Spirit, pulling down strongholds and canceling every demonic strategy formed against us through the power of Jesus Christ. By the authority of His blood and His Word, we stand as warriors, dismantling the enemy's plans and releasing God's victory over our lives and families.

Fast and pray, just as Esther and Daniel did in perilous times
Fasting in prayer, as Esther and Daniel did in times of great peril, humbles us before God and sharpens our spiritual focus. Through this act of consecration, we invite divine intervention, breakthrough, and protection over our lives and nations.

Weapons of Our Warfare

The enemy comes with fear, control, and confusion. But God has given us weapons that are mighty through him.

Your weapons include:

Prayer – Prayer opens the heavens and dispatches angels.

Fasting – Fasting weakens the flesh and strengthens the spirit.

The Word of God – Your sword in battle. Speak it aloud.

Worship – It shifts the atmosphere and silences the enemy.

The Blood of Jesus – The enemy cannot cross the bloodline.

Use your weapons daily. Don't wait until invasion arrives—prepare now.

Angelic Protection and the Lord of Hosts

In the dream, I was hidden from danger—that is the ministry of angels sent by God.

(Psalm 34:7) The angel of the Lord encamped round about them that fear him, and delivered them.

God often sends His angels:

To shield us from what we cannot see.
To stand guard over our children and homes.
To war against demonic assignments.
To lead us out of danger.

You are not alone. The Lord of Hosts—Jehovah Sabaoth—is the Commander of the angelic army, and He assigns angels on behalf of His saints.

Pray

Father in Heaven,

In the mighty name of Jesus Christ, I ask that You dispatch Your holy angels to surround my home, my family, my street, and my city. Let them walk on our behalf in the spiritual realm, standing guard against every scheme of the enemy.

Your Word declares, "The angel of the Lord encamps all around those who fear Him, and delivers them" **(Psalm 34:7, NKJV)**. Therefore, I declare that no weapon formed against us shall prosper **(Isaiah 54:17)**.

Father, let Your angels be as flames of fire **(Hebrews 1:7)**, ministering spirits sent to those who inherit salvation **(Hebrews 1:14)**. Surround our doors, our windows, and our walls, that nothing unclean may enter. Place angelic watchmen over our street and warriors over our city, to war in the heavens on our behalf.

We decree that every demonic assignment is canceled, every stronghold is torn down, and every hidden plan of darkness is exposed and destroyed in the name of Jesus.

Lord, let Your glory fill our homes and neighborhoods, so that peace, righteousness, and protection remain. Just as You placed a hedge of fire around Job **(Job 1:10)**, so place a hedge of protection around us, and let the blood of Jesus cover every entrance. We call forth angelic reinforcements from the north, south, east, and west. We declare that this territory belongs to the Lord. We decree safety, peace, and the covering of Almighty God Amen.

Final Encouragement-Your family is Not Forgotten

In the dream, my greatest concern was for my children. That is the heart of every believer—to see their family saved and protected.

(Isaiah 49:25) For I will contend with him that contendeth with thee, and I will save thy children.

Let this be your declaration:

My children shall live and not die. They will be taught of the Lord. No weapon formed against my family will prosper. I cover them under the blood of Jesus. I stand in the gap for their salvation, deliverance, and purpose.

Even in invasion, there is preservation. Even in judgment, there is mercy.

Hold fast. Stand firm. Keep watching and praying.
Jesus is our shield, and His promises are sure.
Intercession in the Last Days

The dream of soldiers invading homes is a wake-up call to the Church—to rise in intercession.

(Ezekiel 22:30) And I sought for a man among them, that should make up the hedge, and stand in the gap before me for the land.

Intercessors are watchmen who cry out before judgment comes. they discern the times like the sons of Issachar **(1 Chronicles 12:32)**

Pray in the Spirit when they don't know what to say **(Romans 8:26).**

Stand in the gap for family, leaders, and the nation

Now is the time to rise at dawn, lay aside distractions, and press into the secret place. Your prayers can turn back what the enemy planned.

Dreams of Escape and Divine Strategy

In the dream, I was led to hide between the houses—low to the ground—until the danger passed. That posture speaks to humility and obedience.

(James 4:7) Submit yourselves therefore to God. Resist the devil, and he will flee from you.

God gave me a divine strategy. Sometimes protection comes not through confrontation, but through obedient stillness.

In Scripture, God often revealed escape routes:

Joseph was warned in a dream to flee with Mary and Jesus **(Matthew 2:13).**

Lot was told to flee Sodom before destruction **(Genesis 19:15–17).**

The early Church scattered before persecution struck, preserving the Gospel **(Acts 8:1–4).**

Dreams like mine reveal that God is still speaking, still guiding His people to safety.

Preparing the Bride of Christ

The Church is not just a building. She is the Bride of Christ, and she must be ready.

(Revelation 19:7) Let us be glad and rejoice…and give Him glory, for the marriage of the Lamb has comes, and His wife hath made herself ready.

In times of invasion, God is refining His Bride—calling her to:

Repentance

Holiness

Separation from the world

Worship in spirit and truth

This dream reminded me that judgment can begin at the house of God **(1 Peter 4:17).** But those who prepare their garments will be hidden in Christ when the time of trial comes.

Deliverance Is Coming

Though the dream showed a time of war and invasion, it also revealed a truth: God is our Deliverer. **(Psalm 91:3–4)** Surely, he shall deliver thee from the snare of the fowler… He shall cover thee with his feathers, and under his wings shalt thou trust." We do not walk in fear—we walk in faith.

God is raising up deliverers, like Moses and Deborah. He's sending warrior angels, like in Elisha's time **(2 Kings 6:17).**

He's awakening intercessors who will cry out day and night.

Deliverance is not just escape—it's freedom from bondage, victory over fear, and boldness to stand when others faint.

A Call to Watch and Pray

In the dream, I could have run in fear—but I paused, I hid, I prayed. That moment was a picture of what Jesus called us to do: **(Luke 21:36)** Watch ye therefore, and pray always, that ye may be accounted worthy to escape all these things.

To "watch" means to be spiritually alert.
To "pray always" means to have your heart tethered to heaven.

This is not a time to slumber.
This is not a time to compromise.
This is a time to prepare your heart like a wise virgin with oil in her lamp **(Matthew 25:1–13).**

Jesus is coming.
The world is shifting.
The Bride must make herself ready.

God's Covering in the Day of Trouble

In the dream, as the soldiers passed by, I was not seen. Though I was exposed in the natural, I was hidden in the Spirit.

(**Psalm 27:5**) For in the time of trouble he shall hide me in his pavilion: in the secret of his tabernacle shall he hide me.This supernatural covering is not man-made. It is: A hedge of protection like Job had (**Job 1:10**) A divine shadow under the wings of the Almighty (**Psalm 91:1–4**). A mark of God on those who sigh and cry for the sins of the land (**Ezekiel 9:4**). When the destroyer passed through Egypt, those covered by the blood were spared (**Exodus 12**). Likewise, the Lord still marks and hides His people today.

The Hidden Ones

I felt invisible to the invading army—not because of my strength, but because God made me hidden. (**Isaiah 49:2**) And he made me a polished shaft; in his quiver hath he hid me. (**Psalm 83:3**) They have taken crafty counsel... against thy hidden ones. In every generation, God preserves a hidden remnant: Elijah thought he was alone, but God had 7,000 who had not bowed to Baal (**1 Kings 19:18**). During persecution, hidden believers in homes, caves, and forests kept the light burning. Today, watchmen and intercessors are being prepared in secret, ready to be released. The hidden ones are not forgotten—they are being refined in quiet places.

Mothers, Fathers, and the Call to Protect

My heart turned to my children in the dream—I knew they were inside my grandmother's house, and I had to get to them. This was more than natural concern. It was a spiritual burden. (**Nehemiah 4:14**) Fight for your brethren, your sons, and your daughters, your wives, and your houses.

Mothers and fathers are the first intercessors in the home. Our children are not just physical beings, they are arrows in our hands, and spiritual heirs. **(Psalm 127: 3-5)**.

In the last days
Deception will come even to the young **(Matthew 24:24)**
Evil ideologies will target their minds; Spiritual covering must be restored through prayer and teaching. As guardians of our homes, we must become like Noah, preparing an ark of safety for our household **(Hebrews 11:7)**.

The Return to the House

In the dream, once the threat passed, I ran inside to awaken my daughter and gather my children.

This reflects the spiritual urgency we must carry to

Wake up the slumbering Church **(Romans 13:11)**.

Awaken the next generation to their call

Bring the family into spiritual alignment

There's no time for delay!
Like the ten virgins, only those who are ready will enter **(Matthew 25)**. Like the shepherds of old, we must go quickly when heaven warns us. It's time to wake the sleeping daughter—to speak life, declare identity, and point her to the bridegroom.

A Family Altar Must Be Rebuilt

The urgency to get my family together reminds me that the family altar—the place of worship, Word, and prayer—must be restored.

(Joshua 24:15) As for me and my house, we will serve the Lord.

In the chaos of the end times, the ark of safety is not a bunker.
It's not a government program.
It's not a perfect plan.

It is the presence of God dwelling in our homes.

We must:

Read Scripture aloud again

Pray together as families

Speak blessings over our children

Anoint our homes with oil

Declare the blood of Jesus over every doorpost

In times of darkness, God is raising houses of light—families like yours and mine that will stand when others fall.

Chapter 9

The Song of the Innocent

Date of Dream: December 30, 2015

Worship, Innocence, Prophetic Song, God's Voice in Children

Introduction

Throughout scripture, God has often chosen the least likely vessels to reveal His glory—children, the meek, the poor in spirit. This dream is a vivid portrayal of that truth: from the mouth of babes comes a praise so pure, it touches Heaven. On December 30, 2015, I received a dream unlike any other vision of a little boy whose worship unlocked something deep within the spiritual realm.

The Dream

In the dream, I saw a young African American boy, no more than five years old. He lay gently on the floor, arms stretched out by his sides. He wore black slacks and a white, collared, pinstriped shirt—neatly pressed and dignified, almost like attire worn for a holy occasion. His hair was cut low, his skin smooth and brown, and his expression peaceful.

Though he did not move, his mouth was open. And from it came a sound so beautiful, so rich in spirit, that I was captivated. The child began singing a gospel song—a melody I had never heard before in my life. It was not from this world. His voice carried a power and purity that could only come from God. Every word was praise to the Father—

glorifying the Lord Jesus Christ with awe, adoration, and deep reverence.

The song felt like a new song written by the Holy Spirit Himself—a song not taught by man but given from the throne of Heaven. I could feel the atmosphere shift as he sang. I knew I was witnessing something divine, holy, and prophetic: God had placed His voice in a child, and through him, released heavenly praise on the earth.

Interpretation and Revelation

The boy's posture—resting with arm stretched at his sides— could represent complete surrender to God. The purity of his song reflects the kind of worship God desires: worship that is untainted, unlearned by tradition, and birthed through the Spirit.

This dream is a prophetic declaration that God is pouring out His Spirit on all flesh, just as He promised in **(Joel 2:28)**. Even children will prophesy, sing, and worship in divine power. The dream also highlights God's sovereignty to choose unlikely vessels—like this young boy—to release heavenly truths through song and praise.

The "new song" he sang aligns with the worship before the throne in **(Revelation 14:3)** a melody that only the redeemed can understand. His open mouth, filled with spontaneous, Spirit-led worship, shows that God will cause praise to rise from even the youngest and seemingly overlooked voices.

(Joel 2:28) And it shall come to pass afterward, that I will pour out my spirit upon all flesh; and your sons and your daughters shall prophesy.

(Matthew 21:16) Out of the mouth of babes and sucklings thou hast perfected praise.

(Psalm 8:2) Out of the mouth of babes and sucklings hast thou ordained strength.

(Revelation 14:3) And they sung as it were a new song before the throne... and no man could learn that song but the hundred and forty and four thousand.

(Isaiah 11:6) and a little child shall lead them.

Prayer & Reflection —A Prayer of Worship from the Innocent

Heavenly Father,
We thank You that You are raising up a generation of pure-hearted worshipers. Even the youngest among us are being filled with Your Spirit. Let us learn from the little ones—to worship You not with performance, but with purity. Place in our mouths a new song, a heavenly song, birthed in surrender.

Lord Jesus, we honor You. Let our praise be innocent, powerful, and sincere, like that of the child in the dream. We ask You to anoint every child with boldness and truth. May their voices rise to Heaven in worship that shakes the earth.

(Psalm 100:1–2) Make a joyful noise unto the Lord, all ye lands. Serve the Lord with gladness: come before his presence with singing.

(Romans 12:1) Present your bodies a living sacrifice, holy, acceptable unto God, which is your reasonable service.

Prayer & Reflection – A Prayer for a New Song

Father God,
We desire to sing a new song unto You—a melody that rises from the deep places of our spirit, not from rehearsed rituals but from divine encounter. Let Your Holy Spirit release new songs across the earth. Let choirs of angels join with voices of children to worship the Lamb.

Lord, open our mouths, just as You opened the child's in the dream, and fill us with sounds from Heaven. Birth in us a praise that moves mountains and shakes the kingdom of darkness

(Psalm 40:3) And he hath put a new song in my mouth, even praise unto our God: many shall see it, and fear, and shall trust in the Lord.

(Psalm 96:1) O sing unto the Lord a new song: sing unto the Lord, all the earth.

Prayer & Reflection – A Prayer for the Next Generation

Lord God Almighty,
We lift up the children of this generation. May they walk in purity, truth, and boldness. Cover them with Your protection and fill them with Your Spirit. Let them be worshipers, prophets, dreamers, and intercessors.

We declare that children will not be silenced. Their praise will be pure, their voices strong, and their worship holy. May every home be filled with the sound of gospel songs rising from the mouths of the innocent

89

Chapter 10

The Desolation of Moscow, Russia- A Prophetic Warning Dream

Dream Date: August 3, 2016

The Vision Unfolds, It was the early morning hours when I was taken into a vivid dream—one unlike the others, marked by silence, sorrow, and warning. In the vision, I stood in a vast open field. The sky was overcast, with a heavy grayness that pressed against the earth. All around me was stillness. There were no sounds of life—no birds, no breeze, no voices. Just silence. Yet even in the silence, I could feel a scream echoing through the ruins. Something terrible had happened here.

The land stretched far and wide, but it was broken. What might have been buildings now lay crumbled into heaps of ash and stone. The air was thick, not with smoke, but with aftermath— what happens when destruction has already come and gone. It didn't look like a place preparing for war. It looked like a place that had already been judged.

My heart began to race. I felt like a stranger in a foreign land, unaware of how I got there, and unsure of what I was supposed to see. I turned, searching for someone—anyone. That's when I saw her. A woman, running across the open field, moving quickly but with fear in her eyes. Her clothes were torn, her hair unkempt. Her face looked desperate, as if she had witnessed the fall of her homeland. As she neared me, I called out, "Where am I?" Without slowing, she shouted back: "You are in Moscow, Russia."

The name rang loudly in my spirit. Moscow. I looked again at the land around me—devastated, barren, silent. No sign of government, no sign of military, no sign of order. It was as though the city had been emptied, its strength consumed. The once-proud stronghold was now only a shadow of itself. Then I awoke with my soul stirred, and my spirit troubled.

The Weight of the Dream

This dream was more than a scene of destruction. It was a spiritual vision—a divine revelation from the Lord about judgment, war, and the cost of turning away from Him. I knew immediately that this dream carried prophetic weight. The kind of weight that does not pass with time but presses down until it is released through intercession or obedience.

The Lord was revealing not just a place, but a condition of the nations. While Moscow was named, it stood as a symbol of power, pride, and fallen glory. The dream wasn't only about one city—it was a mirror to the world. Any nation that rejects the Lord, exalts itself in pride, or walks in unrighteousness stands at the edge of this same desolation.

Scripture came to my heart as I reflected
"Behold, the Lord maketh the earth empty, and maketh it waste... The land shall be utterly emptied and utterly spoiled: for the Lord hath spoken this word. **(Isaiah 24:1, 3 KJV).**

The ruined buildings represented not just physical war, but spiritual collapse. The field was a battleground where righteousness had once stood, but was now removed. The woman running may represent the remnant—those who still hear God's voice and flee from wrath, calling others to awaken. She may also symbolize the Church, trying to escape judgment after neglecting her prophetic call.

This dream is a call to the intercessors, the prophets, the watchmen, and the Body of Christ to take their place. God is showing what lies ahead—not to bring fear, but to bring repentance and preparation.

Prophetic Layers and Scriptural Parallels

As I continued meditating on the dream, the Spirit of the Lord began to unfold layers of its meaning. What I saw in Moscow was not merely physical desolation—it was a picture of what happens when a nation becomes spiritually barren. It was a warning, not only to Russia but to all nations that lift themselves up in pride, trusting in military might, political power, or human wisdom rather than bowing to the authority of the Living God.

The ruined city in the dream mirrors the warnings of the prophet Jeremiah:

"Because ye have burned incense, and because ye have sinned against the Lord... therefore is this evil happened unto you, as at this day. **(Jeremiah 44:23 KJV).**

Like ancient Babylon, Nineveh, and Jerusalem, modern nations are not exempt from judgment. When the voice of repentance is ignored, when the cries of the righteous are silenced and when the blood of the innocent cries out from the ground, God responds—not always in the moment, but in His perfect timing.

Moscow, a symbol of strength and global influence, appeared empty, shaken, and undone. The silence spoke volumes. It represented a city stripped of its idols, exposed for what it truly was: a nation without God is a nation without foundation.

This aligns with what is written in Proverbs 14:34:

"Righteousness exalteth a nation: but sin is a reproach to any people."

The woman running through the ruins reminds me of Lot fleeing Sodom, and Noah preparing the ark—individuals who responded when the rest of the world mocked or remained blind. In this dream, she carried both urgency and sorrow—perhaps crying out for others to recognize the lateness of the hour. Her message was not just for me, but for the Church, the intercessors, and those who still have ears to hear.

There is a cry from Heaven in this hour:

Return to Me. Awake, O sleeper. Watch and pray. The hour of testing comes upon all nations.

This dream is not meant to incite fear but to provoke repentance, revival, and readiness. It is a clarion call to the Church to rise up in power, to nations to turn from wickedness, and to every believer to stand on the wall and pray for mercy in the land.

The Hour of Reckoning and the Call to Watch The dream of Moscow's desolation was not isolated, it fits into a tapestry of warnings the Lord is releasing in this generation. We are witnessing signs in the heavens, unrest among the nations, and spiritual famine in the land. What I saw in that dream was not just the ruin of a city, but a mirror of what comes when a people reject the voice of God.

The Spirit drew me to the words of the prophet Ezekiel, who was commanded to speak to a rebellious house:

Son of man, when the land sinneth against me by trespassing grievously, then will I stretch out mine hand upon it... and cutoff man and beast from it. **(Ezekiel 14:13 KJV).**

The silence in the dream reminded me of **(Revelation 8:1)**, where there was silence in heaven for about half an hour before the release of the trumpet judgments. That silence is not empty—it is pregnant with divine weight, a pause before the shaking. In the same way, the field I stood in seemed to carry a divine pause. It was not peace. It was the aftermath of judgment and the anticipation of accountability.

I believe this dream is tied to a greater prophetic cycle—a season where God is allowing what can be shaken to be shaken, so that only what is built upon Him will remain **(Hebrews 12:26-27)**. The fall of cities and systems is not the end—it is the mercy of God giving space for repentance before the final hour.

Blow ye the trumpet in Zion and sound an alarm in my holy mountain: let all the inhabitants of the land tremble: for the day of the Lord cometh. **(Joel 2:1 KJV).**

Just as Nineveh was given a chance to repent at the preaching of Jonah, so too are nations being given windows of warning. This dream of Moscow—though bleak—is not without hope. The woman running may symbolize the remnant Church, those who are still crying aloud and sparing not, those who have not bowed to Baal nor kissed him. She was moving. She was awake. She spoke truth: "You are in Moscow, Russia."

She identified the location for a reason. It was not just a spiritual metaphor—it was a prophetic pinpoint, an alert that this message concerns real places, real people, and real consequences.

In this hour, the Lord is calling His people to:

Discern the times **(Matthew 16:3)**

Sound the alarm **(Joel 2:1)**

Stand in the gap **(Ezekiel 22:30)**

Return to the secret place of prayer and fasting **(Matthew 6:6, Joel 2:12-13).**

The desolation I witnessed was sobering, but it was also awakening. It reminded me that this world is passing away, and only those whose lives are hidden in Christ will stand in the day of adversity.

The Remnant's Call – Intercession in the Final Hour

This dream, though short in imagery, carried the weight of prophetic urgency. The barren field in Moscow, the woman running, the city in ruins—all reveal the sobering truth of what lies ahead for nations that continue in rebellion. Yet within this bleakness, the Spirit began to highlight a crucial thread of hope: the rise of the remnant Church.

The woman in the dream did not walk or hide—she ran. She was moving swiftly, aware of time and burdened with message. She represents the watchmen, the intercessors, the hidden warriors of prayer, and the Bride of Christ who refuses to slumber.

Scripture tells us

And it shall come to pass, that whosoever shall call on the name of the Lord shall be delivered: for in Mount Zion and in Jerusalem shall be deliverance... and in the remnant whom the Lord shall call. **(Joel 2:32(KJV).**

It is in the remnant that God's mercy lingers. Even in the face of judgment, the Lord seeks a people who will stand in the gap like Abraham did for Sodom, like Moses did for Israel, and like Daniel did in Babylon. The ruins of Moscow became more than symbolic—they became a global cry for intercession before desolation becomes destiny.

The dream also parallels the end-time narrative in Matthew 24, where Jesus warns of wars, rumors of wars, and desolation in diverse places. He describes a world groaning under the weight of lawlessness and deception, yet within that same chapter, He also gives instruction:

Watch therefore: for ye know not what hour your Lord doth come. **(Matthew 24:42 KJV).**

We are not called passivity. We are called to prophetic watchfulness. The Lord is stirring the hearts of His prophets and dreamers—not for entertainment, but for engagement. The visions, dreams, and divine warnings are not given to be hidden in journals; they are to be shared, prayed over, and released with boldness.

The desolate city in the dream points to a spiritual war zone, perhaps physical war, yes, but also spiritual decay, godlessness, and false security. And yet, like in Revelation 18 where Babylon falls, a voice is heard from heaven saying:

Come out of her, my people, that ye be not partakers of her sins, and that ye receive not of her plagues. **(Revelation 18:4 KJV)**. This dream echoes that cry: Come out. Be separate. Wake up. The hour is late.

Now more than ever, the Church must rise—not just in buildings but on its knees. We must discern the signs, test the spirits, and war in prayer for nations. The desolation can still be halted. Mercy can still prevail—but only if the watchmen blow the trumpet and the people respond.

The Trumpet is Sounding – A Call to Repentance and Intercession

The desolation I saw in the dream is not yet set in stone—it is a warning, a vision of what could come if hearts remain hardened. But the Spirit of God is still calling, still pleading, still searching for those who will stand in the gap.

If my people, which are called by my name, shall humble themselves, and pray, and seek my face, and turn from their wicked ways: then will I hear from heaven, and will forgive their sin, and will heal their land. **(2 Chronicles 7:14 KJV).**

This is not a time for political rhetoric or cultural distractions. It is a time for repentance at the altar, for fasting and weeping between the porch and the altar, as **(Joel 2:17)** declares. God is not looking at buildings or denominations—He is looking at hearts.

In light of the dream, I offer these prophetic prayers and declarations for the remnant to rise and intercede for the nations:

Prayer for the Nations:

Father, in the name of Jesus, we lift up the nations before You. We repent on behalf of those who have forsaken Your Word, who have shed innocent blood, who have made idols of power and pleasure. Let mercy triumph over judgment. Expose every hidden thing and bring leaders, cities, and peoples to their knees in repentance. Send revival fire to Russia, to America, to every land that has turned from You. In wrath, remember mercy. Let Your Spirit be poured out in these last days.

Prayer for the Church:

Awaken Your Bride, O Lord. Shake us from slumber. Remove the fear of man and replace it with holy fear of You. Raise up intercessors, prophets, dreamers, and watchmen who will not rest until righteousness springs forth. Cleanse us from compromise. Let the fire on the altar never burn out. Teach us to watch, to pray, and to prepare the way of the Lord.

Prophetic Declarations:

We declare that the remnant shall not be silenced.

We declare a harvest of souls in Russia and all nations.

We decree that hidden sin shall be exposed and truth will prevail.

We speak life where there has been death, hope where there has been despair, and light where there has been darkness.

We declare that Jesus Christ is Lord over every nation, and His kingdom shall not be moved.

This dream was a trumpet blast—one of many sounding in this hour. Let it be recorded not only in this book but in the hearts of those who will receive it. Let it ignite a flame of holy urgency. Now is the time to cry aloud and spare not. Now is the time to prepare for the Lord.

For the Lord shall arise upon thee, and His glory shall be seen upon thee. And the Gentiles shall come to thy light. **(Isaiah 60:2-3 KJV.)**

Hope After Desolation – Encouragement for the Watchers and Dreamers

Though the dream began in ruins, its message ends with purpose. God does not reveal future devastation to instill fear—He reveals to prepare, to warn, and ultimately to redeem. The vision of a broken Moscow was not the end. It was the beginning of an awakening for the intercessors, a sounding of the alarm for the watchmen to take their place on the walls.

Surely the Lord God will do nothing, but he revealed his secret unto his servants the prophets. **(Amos 3:7 KJV).**

You who are reading this—if God has given you dreams, visions, or burdens for nations—do not dismiss them. Do not keep them hidden in journals. Your voice, your prayers, your obedience could be the spark that shifts an atmosphere. What God reveals to you in secret is often meant to be released with holy boldness.

Even after ruins, God rebuilds. Even after judgment, mercy is extended.

The glory of this latter house shall be greater than of the former, saith the Lord of hosts: and in this place will I give peace. **(Haggai 2:9 KJV).**

Let these words settle into your spirit: Peace will come, but only after repentance. Revival will flow, but only after the Church returns to her first love.

You are not alone. There is a generation rising with fire in their bones—those who carry not just dreams, but destiny. Like Ezekiel in the valley of dry bones, they will speak life into what seems lost. Like Nehemiah, they will rebuild the ruins. Like Esther, they will intercede for their people. Like John on Patmos, they will write what they see—because the time is near.

Write the vision, and make it plain upon tables, so that he may run that readeth it. For the vision is yet for an appointed time. **(Habakkuk 2:2-3 KJV).**

This dream from August 3, 2016, is not just about Moscow—it is a call to the nations, to the Church, and to every believer who hears the Spirit saying, "Come out, wake up, return to Me.

Let us rise as watchmen, as intercessors, as forerunners preparing the way for the King of Glory.

Lift up your heads, O ye gates; and be ye lift up, ye everlasting doors; and the King of glory shall come in. **(Psalm 24:7 KJV)**

A Prophetic Commissioning – Arise and Carry the Mantle

To those who have seen in the spirit.
To those who have dreamed dreams that troubled the night.
To those who have wept in prayer for people they've never met.

This mantle is for you.

You were not chosen because of status, fame, or title. You were chosen because your heart said, "Yes, Lord." And now, the Lord is awakening His end-time army—an unseen remnant, called to watch, to weep, and to warn. You are being commissioned to carry His Word with fire and purity.

And it shall come to pass in the last days, saith God, I will pour out of my Spirit upon all flesh: and your sons and your daughters shall prophesy. **(Acts 2:17 KJV)**

Do not shrink back. Do not silence the voice God placed inside you. Do not be afraid of the faces of men. The hour is late, and the trumpet must sound.

A Prayer of Activation and Blessing

Father, in the name of Jesus,
I lift up every reader whose heart is stirred by this dream, whose spirit burns for the nations, and whose eyes have seen Your signs and wonders in the night. I pray for boldness to rise within them, that they may speak what You reveal, write what You show, and stand when others fall.

Clothe them in humility, shield them with Your Word, and fill them with the fire of the Holy Ghost. Let their mouths become trumpets, their prayers become weapons, and their tears become seeds of revival.

Awaken their gifts. Clarify their vision. Strengthen their feet for the path ahead. Let dreams come with wisdom. Let visions come with interpretation. Let intercession come with authority.

And above all, let Your glory be seen through them—not for fame, but for the harvest, the nations, and the return of the bridegroom.

In Jesus' mighty name, Amen.

Blessed is that servant, whom his lord when he cometh shall find so doing. **(Matthew 24:46 KJV).**

You have been chosen. You have been warned. Now, go forward in obedience.

Let this chapter mark a shift in your life commissioning from heaven for such a time as this.

Chapter 11

The Royal Road: A Sword for the Called

Dream Date: Year 2005

It was the year 2005, in the still hours of the morning when the Spirit of the Lord gave me a dream that I will never forget. I was inside a house during the daytime, when suddenly, there came a knock at the door. Curious, I opened it, and there stood two strangers—a man and a woman. They appeared to be ordinary, dressed in everyday clothing.

Without introducing themselves, they said, "Come with us."

Uncertain and hesitant, I asked, "Where are we going?" I didn't know them, and my spirit questioned their intent. Yet they stepped inside the house as though led by divine permission. A table stood between us, as if it was a boundary or a test. Still, they beckoned me.

Something within me said, "Go." I agreed.

As I stepped outside, the man took my left hand, and the woman took my right. Together, we walked down a narrow road.

On each side of the road, rows of angels knelt in perfect formation. They had swords in their hands, pointed to the ground, and their wings were bowed upward like a canopy of reverence and protection. The atmosphere was holy, radiant, and full of awe.

Then a divine prompting spoke to me: "Look at the ones holding your hands."

When I turned to look, the man and woman were no longer in common clothing. They were now dressed in royalty—he wore kingly garments, and she wore the attire of a queen. I realized I was not walking with ordinary people, but with heavenly messengers sent by God.

Suddenly, I heard a loud sound coming from behind us. Though I could not see its source, the sound shook me. Fear rose up in me, and I ran—straight through the lines of angels.

As I ran, I looked up and saw angels fighting in the sky, swords clashing in brilliant light. The sky was white with clouds, the grass below green like life itself, and the air vibrated with heavenly warfare.

I collapsed to the ground, overcome by the magnitude of what I had witnessed. With my head down, I cried out: "Someone give me a sword! Someone give me a shield so I can fight!"

And just then, a gentle hand reached down—it was the same woman who once seemed ordinary, now clothed in heavenly glory. She lifted me up, and I woke up.

This dream mirrors a divine call and heavenly revelation rooted deeply in Scripture. Let's break down the spiritual meaning through a biblical lens.

The Knock and the Invitation
The dream begins with a knock—echoing **(Revelation 3:20).**

Behold, I stand at the door and knock. If anyone hears My voice and opens the door, I will come in.

God often sends messengers disguised in what seems ordinary. (Hebrews 13:2) reminds us: Do not forget to show hospitality to strangers, for by so doing some have entertained angels without knowing it."

2. The Narrow Road and Angelic Honor Guard
This road symbolizes the path of righteousness. Jesus said in (Matthew 7:14) Narrow is the road that leads to life, and few find it
.

The kneeling angels with swords down represent reverence, readiness, and divine warfare on our behalf (Psalm 91:11).

The Royal Companions
The man and woman's transformation into royalty symbolizes spiritual leadership and heavenly identity. (Revelation 1:6) says: He has made us kings and priests unto God.

The Sound and the Battle Above
The loud unseen force represents the clash of kingdoms—light against darkness. (Ephesians 6:12) explains; For we wrestle not against flesh and blood, but against… spiritual wickedness in high places.

Cry for a Sword and a Shield
This shows the readiness to fight in the spirit. The Word of God is the sword (Ephesians 6:17), and faith is the shield (Ephesians 6:16). I wasn't running from battle—but running into my calling.

The Lifting Hands

God will always send help when we humble ourselves. **(Psalm 18:35)** says: Your right hand sustains me; You stoop down to make me great.

Spiritual Meaning

This dream carries a message not just for me—but for the entire Body of Christ. Here is the prophetic revelation:

God is calling His remnant to step out in faith, even when the direction is unclear.

Heaven is preparing warriors, not spectators. The time of casual Christianity is over.

Angels are positioned—not just for protection but to witness and participate in the warfare of the saints.

You are royalty in the Spirit. Your true- identity is being revealed in this hour.

The cry for a sword and shield is a cry for the Word and the Spirit. God is answering by equipping His people with divine authority.

Fear must be conquered. The battle ahead is not ours but the Lord's, yet He chooses to raise up warriors who will stand with Him.

Spend time meditating on these verses that reflect the heart of this dream:

(Revelation 3:20) Behold, I stand at the door and knock.

(Ephesians 6:10-17) Put on the full armor of God.

(Psalm 91:11) For He shall give His angels charge over you.

(Matthew 7:14) Narrow is the road that leads to life.

(Revelation 1:6) Kings and priests unto God.

(Isaiah 41:10) Fear not, for I am with you.

Prayer of Equipping and Commission

Heavenly Father,
Thank You for the divine call upon my life. Thank You for knocking at the door of my heart and sending Your messengers to lead me. I receive Your calling with humility and reverence. Dress me in Your armor, O God. Place in my hand the sword of the Spirit and cover me with the shield of faith. Remind me that I am not ordinary—I am chosen, set apart, and royal in Your eyes.

Teach me to walk the narrow road with boldness. Let me not be afraid of the sound of battle or the sight of war in the heavens. For You go before me, and Your angels surround me. Lift me when I fall. Equip me when I cry out. And use my life to inspire others to rise, fight, and win for Your glory.
In Jesus' mighty name Amen.

Chapter 12

When Your Feet Get Wet

The Dream (2005)

In a prophetic dream given to me in 2005, I found myself on a boat in the middle of a vast ocean. It was a bright day, and I was standing on the top deck. The boat had two levels—the upper deck where I stood and the lower level which held sleeping quarters.

I wasn't alone. A man was there with me. He had long hair and wore a flowing white robe. His back was to me, so I couldn't see His face. In His hand, He held a saw, and He was working—constructing something on the boat. His presence was holy, peaceful, yet filled with purpose.

Then He spoke:
"When your feet get wet, we will build another boat."

His words stirred something in me. I began to walk around, inspecting the boat, making sure it was sturdy. I even went downstairs to check the sleeping quarters. Everything seemed secure.

When I returned to the top deck, He repeated:
"When your feet get wet, we will build another boat."

As I looked out into the ocean, I saw how far I was from the land. The shoreline was distant, and the people on

It looked like tiny specks. But I could see children running across the white sand, joyfully shouting: "Jesus! Jesus! Jesus!"

Then I noticed a man swimming near the boat—he was struggling, close to drowning. My heart was moved. I cried out, "Lord, hand me the saw so I can start helping!"

Once again, the man in the robe said:
"When your feet get wet, we will build another boat."

And then I woke up.

Spiritual Revelation and Biblical Interpretation

This was not just a dream — it was a divine instruction.

The boat represents a place of safety, preparation, and spiritual responsibility. God was showing me that I was already on a vessel of calling, equipped and ready — yet I had not yet stepped into the water. The man in the white robe—a clear symbol of Jesus—was already working, building, preparing the next assignment. And yet, He was waiting for me to respond in action.

The repeated words,
"When your feet get wet, we will build another boat,"
hold prophetic weight. God was saying:

"When you step out of your comfort zone, when you leave the place of security, when you move beyond just watching and start walking by faith into the unknown — then I will multiply your purpose. Then I will build through you."

The man swimming near the boat represented the lost, the broken, the struggling souls who are barely keeping afloat in life. They are within reach — but unless someone gets their feet wet, they may drown. Your willingness to help, your desire for the saw, reveals your heart: ready to partner with Christ in the work of salvation and restoration.

The children on the white sand, shouting "Jesus," represent the next generation, or those coming into spiritual awakening. They are calling for the Lord, and they need laborers who are willing to launch out from the safety of the boat and reach them.

Message to You, Dear Reader
This dream is not just for me. It is for you too.
You may be on your own "boat" right now — living in a place of observation or preparation. Perhaps you've been watching from a distance, examining your faith, testing the waters, making sure everything is secure before stepping out.

But listen:
The Lord is calling you.
He's saying, "When your feet get wet, we will build another boat."

He's inviting you to leave the comfort of the deck and step into the waters of purpose. The sea may look deep, and the land may seem far away, but you are not alone. Christ is on the boat. He has the tools. He is ready to build through you, but He's waiting for your step of faith.

The lost are within reach.
There are souls swimming near your boat—hurting, drowning, crying out. Will you extend your hand? Will you ask for the saw and begin to build?

The children are calling "Jesus"—and God wants to send you to answer them. You are a carrier of the gospel. You are a builder of refuge. But it starts when your feet get wet.

Scriptures to Meditate On
(Luke 5:4) Launch out into the deep. God is calling you deeper.

(Matthew 14:29) So He said, 'Come.' And Peter came down out of the boat. Jesus calls you to walk where fear says you can't.

(Isaiah 6:8) Here am I, send me! Let this be your response to His calling.

Proverbs 24:11 – "Rescue those being led away to death..."
You are called to help save others.

(Ephesians 2:10) Created for good works. You were made for this mission.

(Hebrews 11:7) By faith, Noah prepared an ark.
You are a builder in this generation.

Heavenly Father, in the name of Jesus, I pray for the one reading this now. Stir their heart to action. Let them not be content watching from the deck. Give them the courage to step into the waters of faith. Equip them with the tools of Your Spirit — wisdom, love, and power. Let them see the drowning souls and respond with boldness. May they hear Your voice saying, "When your feet get wet, we will build another boat. "And may they say, "Yes, Lord. Send me." In Jesus' name, Amen.

111

Chapter 13

The Heavenly Construction Dream

Dream Year (2005)

In 2005, I had a powerful and unforgettable dream that felt more real than waking life. It began in a check-cashing place, where I stood in line with my middle son. He was playful and energetic, like any young child. As always, I was alert, scanning my surroundings.

Suddenly, a man stormed in carrying a sawed-off shotgun. He moved swiftly and with purpose, heading directly into the cashier's area through a slightly ajar door. The scene erupted into chaos. As I turned, I saw someone throw a paper sack over my son's head, as if to abduct him. Panic gripped my heart.

Then something miraculous happened. My body began lifting upward—I was ascending. I rose higher and higher, passing through the ceiling, then the roof, until I was above the building. I looked down and saw turmoil: people screaming, police rushing in, ambulances arriving confusion everywhere. Yet as I continued ascending, a single tear rolled from my eye for the child I thought I had lost. But that sorrow was soon overtaken by overwhelming peace, joy, and divine calm.

While I floated in the sky, the sack was removed from the child—and it wasn't my son anymore. It was my daughter.

This shift didn't confuse me; instead, I felt God was showing me something symbolic.

Suddenly, I became aware of the presence beside me. Though I couldn't see His face, I knew deep in my soul—it was Jesus. He flew beside me through the sky. He was speaking, but I couldn't hear Him with my ears—only my spirit was aware of His words. Still, His presence brought deep comfort and a knowing that I was safe.

As we soared together, I saw a magnificent gate ahead. It opened as we approached, and we entered what I can only describe as a heavenly city in the process of construction. The scene was bustling, not with chaos, but with divine purpose. Bulldozers were scooping up dirt and hurling it into the air, and as the dirt fell, it transformed into buildings—high-rises, condominiums, individual homes, and structures too marvelous to describe. It was as if the soil obeyed the will of heaven.

The ground beneath was vibrant with life. Flowers in colors I cannot name swayed gently, as though they were singing. Their movement and color felt alive—expressing praise, perhaps.

As Jesus guided me through the city, I watched everything with awe. He continued speaking, and though I couldn't hear the words, I felt their meaning: this city was not yet complete. It was being built for those who believe in Him—for those who are coming home.

Eventually, we exited the heavenly gate, and I began descending again. The light grew brighter, and I saw the Earth below. Jesus gently placed me on red clay dirt—the kind I remembered from my childhood, where our family's country church once stood.

He pointed and said, "This is your house." Before me appeared a beautiful white home.

Then He said, "This is your land." I saw a vast expanse of green fields and many other white houses scattered around, like a community of the redeemed.

Finally, He said, "I love you." A single, giant tear fell from the sky and splashed upon the ground. I felt it—not just physically, but deep in my soul. His words stirred me to my core.

I cried out, "Jesus, I love You!"

Then I looked down—and I was no longer standing on clay. I stood upon a solid rock.

And I woke up.

Biblical Insights and Interpretations

The Ascent Above Chaos: Symbolic of the rapture or divine deliverance from earthly turmoil. Then we who are alive and remain shall be caught up... to meet the Lord in the air. **(1 (Thessalonians 4:17).**

Jesus' Silent Presence: His love speaks even when words are unspoken. My sheep hear My voice... and they follow Me. **(John 10:27).**

Heaven in Progress: Reflects His promise.
In My Father's house are many mansions... I go to prepare a place for you. **(John 14:2-3).**

Red Clay turn into a Solid Rock: Represents transformation and spiritual stability.
He... set my feet on a rock. **(Psalm 40:2).**

Jesus' Tear: A sign of divine love and empathy.
"He will wipe away every tear. **(Revelation 21:4).**

Jesus Saying "I Love You": The core of the Gospel.
But God demonstrates His own love for us... Christ died for us. **(Romans 5:8).**

As I descended slowly from the brilliance of that heavenly place, I felt the weight of Earth returning—but this time, I carried something different. The light of the city, the peace in Jesus' presence, and the sight of the homes prepared for the redeemed—it all stayed within me. Though I was no longer floating through the sky, my spirit was still soaring.

When my feet touched the red clay again, I realized I wasn't alone. All around me, I could sense others who had once walked through this same soil. Saints who prayed on this land, cried on this land, believed on this land. Though I couldn't see them with my eyes, I felt connected to a spiritual legacy—those who had lived in faith before me. It was as though God was saying, "This is sacred ground."

That little white country church I remembered from my childhood wasn't visible in the dream, but I knew it had once stood nearby. Memories flooded back of hymns sung in that old wooden buildings, songs about the sweet by and by, the mansion over the hilltop, and the promised land. And now, I had seen with my own eyes that those songs weren't just poetry. They were prophecy.

As I stood in silence, I looked again at the beautiful white home Jesus had shown me. Its roof shimmered with a pearlescent glow, and its windows gleamed like crystal. It wasn't large or extravagant by earthly standards, but it radiated purity, purpose, and peace. I knew it was mine—not earned by work but given by grace.

Then I noticed something powerful: there were no shadows. No corners dimmed by darkness, no fear lurking nearby. Everything was fully known and fully lit. I realized that in this place, nothing was hidden—only truth dwelt there. The kind of truth that doesn't expose to shame but exposes to heal. Every part of the land breathed with holiness, as though heaven's breath flowed through it.

And then, I heard His voice—not through ears, but through spirit—clearer this time:

"Tell them what you saw. Tell them I am real. Tell them I am coming."

A holy urgency filled my soul. It wasn't fear—it was fire. A mission had been deposited into my spirit. This dream wasn't just a comfort—it was a call. I understood that what I had witnessed wasn't just for me. It was a glimpse meant to awaken hearts, to stir souls to seek Jesus while there is still time.

When I awoke, I didn't want to move. The tears I had cried in the dream were still wet on my face. I whispered His name, "Jesus," and the atmosphere in my room still carried the scent of glory.

Even now, I carry this vision like a torch. Every hardship I've faced since then, every loss or battle, I've faced it remembering: this world is not my home. The chaos of this Life is temporary. But Jesus—He is eternal. His city is real. And it is being prepared even now. One day, the gate will open again. And this time, it won't be a dream. It will be forever.

Prayer of Reflection

Heavenly Father,
Thank You for showing us glimpses of Your glory and the place You are preparing for those who love You. Even in the face of fear and chaos, You lift us to a higher place of peace. Jesus, thank You for being with me—even when I can't hear Your voice, I know You are near.

Plant my feet on the solid rock of Your Word. Help me to live in faith, always looking forward to the day when You welcome me into that heavenly city.

I receive Your love, and I return it with my whole heart.
Prepare my heart, Lord, and make me ready.
In Jesus' name, Amen.

Chapter 14

The Garden Encounter A Dream from 1985

In the year 1985, when I was just sixteen years old, I had a powerful and life-changing dream that I now recognize as a divine encounter.

In the dream, I found myself standing in what I knew to be the Garden of Eden. The air was filled with peace and wonder. Towering green trees rustled softly in the breeze, their leaves shimmering like emeralds under the glory of God. Flowers bloomed in vibrant 9hues, and the ground seemed to pulse with life. There was no fear, no sorrow, only a radiant calmness that words cannot fully describe.

In the midst of this paradise, I saw a marble bench. It was pure white, gleaming, and bathed in a brilliant light coming from above. As I looked closer, I noticed a little girl, no older than four or five, kneeling in front of the bench with her hands folded in prayer. She was wrapped in innocence and peace. As I observed her, drawn by the purity of the moment, I suddenly realized something astonishing—that little girl was me.

Then I heard a voice. It was not loud, but it was clear, authoritative, and full of love. The voice said:

"Little girl, little girl, you pray all the time, but you're missing a piece."

Suddenly, a hand came down from heaven. It was robed in a white cloth—pure and holy. In the palm of this heavenly hand was a white marble triangle-shaped stone. The hand extended toward me and placed the stone in my hands.

At that very moment, I woke up.

Biblical Insight and Interpretation

This dream is rich with symbolism and divine instruction:

The Garden of Eden symbolizes the presence of God, the place where humanity was originally designed to walk in perfect communion with Him. **(Genesis 2:8-9).**

The little girl praying represents the purity and sincerity of prayer. Jesus said, "Truly I tell you, unless you change and become like little children, you will never enter the kingdom of heaven. **(Matthew 18:3).**

The voice from heaven highlights that even in our deep spiritual practices, we can still be missing a key part of God's purpose for us. Revelation comes in layers. **(1 Corinthians 13:12).**

The triangle-shaped stone could symbolize the Trinity—Father, Son, and Holy Spirit—and God's completeness being imparted into my life. Jesus is also referred to as the "cornerstone" **(Ephesians 2:20)**, a foundational piece.

The phrase "you are missing a piece" echoes God's desire for us not just to be religious or prayerful, but to be whole, filled with His Spirit and walking in full purpose.

Scriptures for Reflection

(Jeremiah 29:13) You will seek me and find me when you seek me with all your heart.

(Proverbs 3:5-6) Trust in the Lord with all your heart and lean not on your own understanding; in all your ways submit to him, and he will make your paths straight.

(1 Peter 2:5) You also, like living stones, are being built into a spiritual house.

(Isaiah 28:16) See, I lay a stone in Zion, a tested stone, a precious cornerstone for a sure foundation.

(Philippians 1:6) He who began a good work in you will carry it on to completion until the day of Christ Jesus.

Heavenly Father,
I lift up every reader of this testimony and dream. Lord, just as You spoke to me in the innocence of my youth, I ask that You speak to them today. Shine Your light into the gardens of their hearts. Show them what piece may be missing—not in condemnation, but in love.

Reveal Yourself, Lord, with clarity and truth. May Your holy hand reach down into their lives with Your divine cornerstone—Jesus Christ. Complete every area that feels lacking. Heal every wound. Renew their joy and purpose. Fill them with Your Spirit.

Let them hear Your voice say, "You pray all the time, but you're missing a piece," and let them receive that missing piece now in the mighty name of Jesus.
Amen.

This dream is a reminder that God sees our devotion, hears our prayers, and still wants to give us more—not just what we ask for, but what we don't even realize we need.

Let this word stir your heart. Ask the Lord today:
"What piece am I missing, Lord?"
And trust Him to answer in love.

Continuing the Journey: Seeking the Missing Piece

Dear Reader,
If you have ever felt that your prayers seem routine or that your spiritual life is somehow incomplete, you are not alone. Many believers earnestly seek God, yet there remains a quiet whisper in their hearts—a sense that something more is needed, something deeper than words alone.

The dream I had in the Garden of Eden reveals a profound truth: God desires intimacy with us beyond just the act of praying. He longs to give us the missing piece that will complete the spiritual picture He began painting at the moment of our salvation.

What is this missing piece?

It might be different for each of us, but the Bible gives us clues. The missing piece could be:

A deeper revelation of God's love and grace **(Ephesians 3:18-19)**.

The infilling of the Holy Spirit, empowering us to live fully **(Acts 1:8)**.

Healing from past wounds and brokenness **(Psalm 147:3).**

A renewed purpose or calling to serve in His kingdom **(Jeremiah 1:5).**

A greater surrender and trust that opens the door to God's fullness **(Romans 12:1-2).**

God's hand extended that white triangular stone—symbolizing stability, unity, and perfection—not just as a gift, but as an invitation.

An Invitation to Reflect and Respond:

Take a moment now to reflect on your spiritual journey. Ask yourself:

Am I truly seeking God with my whole heart, or have I grown comfortable in the routine?

Is there an area in my life where I feel incomplete or disconnected from God?

Am I open to receiving something new, even if it challenges my current understanding?

Remember, God never forces Himself upon us. Like the hand in the dream, He gently offers His gift. It is up to us to receive it.

Father God, Today I come before You with an open heart. I surrender the parts of me that are closed or fearful. I ask You to reveal to me the piece I am missing—the piece that will make me whole in You. Fill me with Your Spirit. Heal my wounds. Renew my passion for You. Guide my steps and help me to trust Your perfect timing and purpose. May I never settle for less than Your fullness. Help me to walk each day in the joy and peace that only You can give. In Jesus' name, Amen.

Your Next Step

If you feel stirred by this message, consider spending time in prayer and Scripture, asking God for clarity about your missing piece. Surround yourself with believers who can support and encourage you. Be open to God's timing and His ways—often, the most profound growth happens in the waiting.

Remember, just as a small marble stone can be a foundation piece in a building, the smallest revelation from God can become the cornerstone of your spiritual life.

You are on a sacred journey. Keep walking. Keep praying. And keep looking to the One who holds all pieces in His hands.

Bible Study Questions

1. What does the Garden of Eden symbolize in Scripture, and how does it relate to your personal relationship with God? **(Genesis 2:8-9; Revelation 2:7).**

2. Jesus said we must become like little children to enter the Kingdom of Heaven. What qualities of a child can you embrace more in your faith? **(Matthew 18:3-4).**

3. What does it mean to be "built into a spiritual house" with living stones? How might you be a living stone in God's kingdom? **(1 Peter 2:4-5: Ephesians 2:19-22).**

The voice said, "You pray all the time but you're missing a piece." What might this "missing piece" be for you personally? How can you seek it?**(Jeremiah 29:13; Proverbs 3:5-6)**

5. How does understanding Trinity (Father, Son, Holy Spirit) bring completeness to your faith? How can focus on the Trinity help you find the missing piece?
(Matthew 28:19; John 14:16-17).

6. What steps can you take to invite God's fullness into your life and receive the gift He is offering?
(Acts 1:8; Romans 12:1-2).

7. Describe your current prayer life. Do you feel it is routine, vibrant, or somewhere in between? What would you like to change or grow?

8. Reflect on the "missing piece" that God might be pointing to in your life. Write down 2 thoughts, feelings, or impressions you sense He is revealing to you.

9. Write a prayer asking God to show you this missing piece and to help you receive His gift fully and without hesitation.

10. Think about a time when God surprised you with a blessing or insight that you weren't expecting. How did it change your faith?

11. What childlike qualities do you want to cultivate more in your walk with God? How can these qualities help you grow closer to Him?

12. Make a list of practical ways you can deepen your relationship with God this week—such as Scripture reading,

worship, fellowship, or serving others. "How Can You Save Jesus?" — A Resurrection Dream (1991)

On Easter Sunday in 1991, I fell asleep with a heavy question in my heart:

"Why didn't they save Jesus?"

As I drifted off, I found myself suddenly walking through with goods of that ancient time. I walked into one specific what looked like a biblical marketplace — dusty streets lined with people, vibrant voices echoing, and shops filled shop that caught my attention. Ropes hung from wooden beams like vines, and beautiful blue and white hair bows were delicately tied to them. Mixed in with the bows were tallit prayer shawls, also blue and white — symbolic of Jewish tradition and reverence **(Numbers 15:38-40)**.

Drawn to their beauty, I took one of the bows and tied it gently in my hair.

As I did, a voice broke through the market noise — strong and full of authority:
"How can you save Jesus?"

Startled, I turned around. There stood a man unlike any I'd ever seen. He had a long white beard that flowed past his knees to his toes, and his presence radiated peace and wisdom. He looked straight into my soul. Trying to lighten the moment, I answered half-jokingly, "By faith? "He shook his head slowly and Said No." Then I paused, thought deeper, and responded again, "By grace?" His eyes lit up, and with a smile he said, "Yes. Well done."

He embraced me with a warm, approving hug. Then I turned and noticed a bench nearby — and seated on it were what appeared to be the disciples of Jesus. Each one stood to greet me with open arms and embraced me with joy, as if welcoming a sister in faith. The entire atmosphere was bright, almost heavenly, filled with sunlight and divine peace. Then I woke up.

Interpretation and Biblical Meaning.

This dream carries profound biblical truth and personal revelation. Let's break it down:

The Marketplace Setting

The marketplace reflects the world, busy with trade, distractions, and culture. Yet, amidst it, you sought spiritual beauty — the blue and white bows and tallits symbolize truth, revelation, and covenant with God **(Exodus 28:5; Numbers 15:38).**

The Question: "How Can You Save Jesus?"

This was the cry of your soul — wanting to protect or redeem the suffering Christ. But the reality is He came to save us, not the other way around **(John 3:16-17)**.

(Ephesians 2:8-9 NIV):

"For it is by grace you have been saved, through faith — and this is not from yourselves, it is the gift of God — not by works, so that no one can boast."

I realize I was given a spiritual riddle — a question that led to divine truth. My first answer, "by faith," was good — but not complete without grace. Faith is the vessel, but grace is the power.

The Man with the White Beard

He represents wisdom, the Ancient of Days **(Daniel 7:9)**, possibly a heavenly messenger or even a representation of the Lord Himself. His beard and embrace speak of eternal love and approval.

The Embrace of the Disciples

Their hugs were symbolic of spiritual acceptance — the cloud of witnesses welcoming me into deeper understanding and fellowship in Christ (Hebrews 12:1, Luke 22:29-30). It was confirmation that I was walking in truth and revelation.

Message to the Reader

You may be carrying deep questions like,
"Could I have done more for Jesus?"
"Am I worthy of His love?"
The truth is: Jesus did it all for you.

You can't save Jesus — He came to save you. Not by your work, but by His grace alone. Just like the dreamer, perhaps you've been trying to earn God's love through actions. But today, I received this truth:

(Titus 3:5 NIV): "He saved us, not because of righteous things we had done, but because of His mercy." Let the bows, the colors, the hug, and the light remind you — you are seen, chosen, and embraced.

Prayer and Decree
Heavenly Father,
Thank You for the gift of dreams and divine encounters. Just as You spoke through this Easter dream, I ask that You reveal Your grace more deeply to all who read this testimony.

127

I repent of trying to earn what You have freely given. I receive Your grace, Your love, and Your embrace.

Lord, help me understand that my salvation is not by might, not by power, but by Your Spirit and grace **(Zechariah 4:6)**.
I declare that I am saved, loved, and welcomed into Your kingdom not by my strength, but by the blood of Jesus Christ.

I Decree

I am saved by grace through faith.

I walk in divine favor and acceptance.

The enemy cannot accuse me, for I am covered by the Lamb.

I will no longer strive to earn God's love — I will rest in it.

I am hugged by heaven, seated with the saints, and called by name.

In the mighty name of Jesus, Amen.

Christ, Our Anchor in the Storm

This hope we have as an anchor of the soul, both sure and steadfast, and which enters the Presence behind the veil.
(Hebrews 6:19, NKJV)

In the chaos of life—when trials, rage and peace seem out of reach—we need something steady. That "something" is Jesus Christ. He is our Anchor: not drifting, not wavering, but firm and steadfast.

When everything else is changing, Christ remains the same. The anchor of our soul reaches beyond emotion and circumstance into the very presence of God, secured by Christ's atoning blood. You are not held by your own strength, but by His unwavering covenant.

Prayer

Lord Jesus, thank You for being my anchor when life feels out of control. Teach me to rest in Your unchanging love. Help me place my trust in You every day. Amen.

Reflection Questions

1. What storms are you facing right now?

2. Are you anchored to Christ—or something temporary?

Describe a moment in your life when you felt unstable. How did God show you that He was still holding you?

Stability in a Shifting World

Heaven and earth will pass away, but My words will by no means pass away. **(Matthew 24:35, NKJV).**

But everyone who hears these sayings of Mine, and does them, I will liken him to a wise man who built his house on the rock. **(Matthew 7:24, NKJV).**

Jesus teaches that when we build on His Word, we build on rock. In contrast, the world is unstable. Politics, finances, and emotions shift—but God's Word never fails.

Living by truth gives you stability that feelings can't provide. The world changes, but the Rock remains. Even when the rain descends and the floods rise, your soul can stand tall.

Prayer

God, teach me to build my life on Your Word. Let every decision, every plan, every hope be grounded in You. I choose to trust Your eternal truth over temporary noise. Amen.

Reflection Questions

1. What are you building your life on?

2. How can you incorporate God's Word into your daily choices?

Write about a time when God's Word gave you peace or direction. How did it change your outcome?

Security in His Presence

The name of the Lord is a strong tower; the righteous run to it and are safe. **(Proverbs 18:10, NKJV).**

God is our refuge and strength, a very present help in trouble. **(Psalm 46:1, NKJV).**

The presence of Jesus doesn't just calm the storm—it calms you. You are not safe because the danger disappears, but because you are hidden in Him.

There is peace in knowing that no enemy can snatch you from His hand (John 10:28). There is security in His voice, His presence, and His promises. Run into the tower of His name— and find safety there.

Prayer

Lord, I run to You today. You are my hiding place and my strong tower. In You, I am safe. Guard my heart, calm my fears, and cover my mind with Your truth. Amen.

Reflection Questions

1. Do you feel safe in God's presence?

2. What do you run to when fear strikes?

List the names of God that bring you comfort (e.g., Refuge, Father, Deliverer). What does each one mean to you?

Anchored by Grace and Truth

My grace is sufficient for you, for My strength is made perfect in weakness. **(2 Corinthians 12:9, NKJV)**.

And of His fullness we have all received, and grace for grace. **(John 1:16, NKJV)**.

Even when we fall, the Anchor holds. Even when we are weak, He is strong. Christ holds us by grace—not perfection.

His truth doesn't shame—it restores. His grace doesn't excuse sin—it breaks chains. We are anchored not because of our righteousness, but because of His mercy.

Prayer
Jesus, thank You for grace. Thank You that when I drift, You pull me back. I don't deserve it, but I receive it. Anchor me in Your love, and teach me to walk in both grace and truth. Amen.

Reflection Questions

1. Where have you seen God's grace in your life?

2. Are you letting past failures define you—or are you anchored in His mercy?

Write a letter to Jesus, thanking Him for a time when He pulled you back from a place you thought you couldn't return from.

Holding Fast Until the End

Let us hold fast the confession of our hope without wavering, for He who promised is faithful. **(Hebrews 10:23, NKJV)**.

Now to Him who is able to keep you from stumbling, and to present you faultless. **(Jude 1:24, NKJV)**.

God didn't bring you this far to leave you now. He is faithful to finish what He started. Keep holding fast to His promises, even when things get hard.

Jesus is not only the Anchor in your storm—He is the Author and Finisher of your faith **(Hebrews 12:2)**. He holds you, strengthens you, and will never let go.

Prayer
Faithful God, give me strength to hold on. I believe that You are finishing the work You began in me. Help me endure to the end, fully anchored in Your love. Amen.

Reflection Questions

1. Are you weary in your walk with Christ?

2. What promise are you holding onto right now?

Declare in writing: "I will hold fast because God is faithful." Then list the promises from His Word that strengthen you to keep going.

Closing Note to the Reader

You are not drifting aimlessly—you are anchored in Christ. Storms may come, but your soul is secure. He is your Rock, your Refuge, your Redeemer. Drop your anchor in Him daily, and you will never be moved.

Chapter 15

The Daughter and the King

Dream Date: March 25, 2020 – 8:00 a.m.

I awoke from a dream that left a deep impression on my spirit. In the dream, I saw my daughter, radiant and peaceful, married to a king. He was young, noble, and burdened with responsibility. The setting was grand, yet solemn, as the king was preparing for a series of important speeches. My daughter, now queen, stood beside him with grace and quiet strength, helping him dress, girding him in royal garments. She wasn't just his wife; she was his helper, his support, and his comforter.

As I watched, I asked the king, "Where is your royal robe?" His response was unexpected: "I already wore it," he said. "Now, I must prepare for the rest of my speeches." There was something sorrowful in his tone, as though the robe—symbolizing authority, inheritance, or even anointing—had already served its purpose, and greater duties awaited him.

I noticed something deeper. The king did not seem eager to hold this crown. He looked as though the throne had been thrust upon him—not sought, but submitted to, out of obedience to his father. There was an invisible pressure, a sense that his reign was part of a legacy, but not his personal desire.

Nearby stood his brother, whose countenance was tinged with jealousy. It was subtle but telling. His eyes seemed to question why the crown was not his. In that moment, I felt the weight of many things happening behind the scenes—spiritual tensions, family dynamics, and destiny unfolding. Then I woke up.

Spiritual and Biblical Insights for the Reader

Dear reader, this dream holds profound spiritual symbolism. It reveals more than just a royal narrative—it is a divine message about spiritual inheritance, obedience, calling, and the role of godly alignment in leadership.

The king represents one who has been chosen by divine appointment, not ambition. Just as David was anointed king while still a shepherd boy **(1 Samuel 16:11-13)**, not by personal desire but by God's sovereign will, this king was called to a role he did not chase. He is a picture of Christ-like obedience, doing the will of the Father, not seeking His own glory **(John 6:38)**.

The daughter, now queen, reflects the role of the bride of Christ—the Church—who supports and prepares the King's way. She reflects the description in **(Proverbs 31:11-12)**: "The heart of her husband safely trusts her... she does him good and not evil all the days of her life." She also mirrors Esther, who was divinely positioned beside the king "for such a time as this" **(Esther 4:14)**, prepared to influence and help carry out God's plan. When the king says, "I already wore the robe," it echoes a transition—perhaps from the season of preparation to manifestation, or from glory to greater responsibility. It reminds us of **(Philippians 2:6-8)**, where Christ laid aside His glory to fulfill the mission of salvation. The brother's jealousy reflects the spirit of Cain **(Genesis 4:5-8)** or Esau **(Genesis 27)**—those who feel entitled to a blessing but fail to understand the cost of spiritual obedience.

The king's burdened spirit teaches us that true leadership in the Kingdom is weighty. It is not about titles or robes, but about service, sacrifice, and purpose. Jesus said, "Whoever desires to be great among you, let him be your servant" **(Matthew 20:26).**

If you find yourself connected to this dream—whether as the daughter, the king, or the watching parent—ask yourself: What is God preparing you for? Are you called to stand beside someone carrying a heavy assignment? Are you being prepared for a crown you didn't ask for, yet God ordained? Or are you watching from a distance, unaware that you, too, have a role to play in this royal journey?

This dream reminds us that God elevates the humble and uses the unlikely. The path to kingship, or spiritual maturity, often comes with burdens, not applause. But to those who say yes, there is grace, there is covering, and there is eternal reward **(2 Timothy 4:8).**

Let this dream stir your heart. God is preparing His sons and daughters—not just for earthly titles—but for Kingdom reign. May we be found faithful in our season of preparation.

A Prayer of Divine Preparation and Obedience

Heavenly Father,
We come before You with hearts open, humbled by the mystery of Your calling. Thank You for the revelation hidden in dreams—divine messages that prepare our spirits for the path ahead. Just as You chose David, Esther, and Joseph, You are still choosing Your servants today—those who will walk in obedience, not out of personal ambition, but out of deep surrender to Your will.

Lord, prepare us for the royal garments You have assigned. Whether we are called to lead, to serve beside a leader, or to watch and intercede, help us recognize the weight and worth of our position in Your Kingdom. We ask for the spirit of humility, that we may not envy another's crown, but trust You for our own portion and timing.

Teach us, Father, not to seek the robe for the sake of recognition, but to carry Your message, to speak when You say speak, and to remain still when You say wait. Let us never forget that true kingship begins in servanthood, and true glory comes through surrender.

Lord, if we are the ones being prepared like Esther, clothe us in wisdom, purity, and grace. If we are like the king in the dream, give us strength to obey the father's will even when it feels heavy. And if we are the observer, like a watchman on the wall, give us discernment to recognize divine movement and intercede in love and truth.

We surrender to Your perfect plan. Equip us, anoint us, and align us with Heaven's design. Let jealousy, fear, or confusion never distract us from our destiny. Instead, may we walk boldly into the royal purpose for which we were born.
In Jesus' mighty and sovereign name, we pray,
Amen.

Under His Wings A Dream of Covering and Calling

Dream Date: June 12, 2025
Dreamer By Daughter Maria

The Dream – A Divine Encounter

In the dream, my daughter stood outside in an open space. The skies above were clear and peaceful. Then she noticed a majestic, radiant bird flying gracefully in circles around her. Its feathers were filled with vibrant colors, almost like a rainbow woven into wings. There was something heavenly about this bird—its beauty was unmatched, and it radiated an otherworldly glory.

Standing nearby was a girl—she felt like a friend, though my daughter wasn't quite sure if she actually knew her. The girl wore a long, colorful coat, and its pattern was identical to the bird's feathers. The moment the bird saw her, it landed on her shoulder and refused to leave. It stayed with her as if it recognized her.

My daughter then said aloud, "Maybe it thinks you're another bird because your coat looks like its feathers."

In that moment, the great bird flew toward my daughter. Its large wings flapped right in front of her face, stirring the air like a strong wind. She felt the overwhelming presence and instinctively knelt.

As she knelt, the bird took its white claws—or hands—and gently gripped her shoulders. Then it did something extraordinary: it spread its wings wide and wrapped them around her, as though covering her with divine protection. She felt as if the bird was preparing to lift her off the ground—to carry her somewhere higher.

Suddenly, the scene changed. She was now sitting at a desk in a school, quietly doing math work, focused and determined. Then she awoke.

Let's break down the dream to unlock its deeper spiritual message—not only for my daughter, but for you, the reader.

The Colorful Bird — The Holy Spirit in His Glory

This bird is not ordinary creature. It is symbolic of the Holy Spirit—majestic, multi-dimensional, full of beauty and mystery. The many colors of its feathers mirror the sevenfold Spirit of God **(Isaiah 11:2)**, the gifts of the Spirit **(1 Corinthians 12),** and the multifaceted nature of God's glory.

The bird's choice to land on the girl in the colorful coat reveals a spiritual truth: The Holy Spirit rests upon those who reflect His image.

"And the Spirit of the Lord shall rest upon Him, the Spirit of wisdom and understanding, the Spirit of counsel and might, the Spirit of knowledge and of the fear of the Lord." **(Isaiah 11:2).**

"Then John bore witness, saying, 'I saw the Spirit descending from heaven like a dove, and He remained upon Him." **(John 1:32).**

The Colorful Coat — Divine Identity and Favor

Just as Joseph's coat of many colors marked him as favored and chosen **(Genesis 37:3),** so this girl's coat identified her as someone the Spirit recognizes. She may represent people in your life—friends, mentors, or even yourself—who wear the "mark" of God's anointing, though you may not fully understand it yet. The matching of the coat and bird speaks of oneness—of being in step with the Spirit.

For as many as are led by the Spirit of God, these are sons of God. **(Romans 8:14).**

The Kneeling – Surrender and Humility

When my daughter knelt, she entered a position of submission. She didn't run or resist. She knelt. This is the posture God is calling many of us into. It is the place where elevation begins.

Humble yourselves in the sight of the Lord, and He will lift you up. **(James 4:10).**

The Covering Wings – Divine Protection and Transformation

The bird's wings wrapping around her shoulders symbolize covering, safety, and a personal encounter with the Holy Spirit. His wings not only protect but impart strength.

He shall cover you with His feathers, and under His wings you shall take refuge. **(Psalm 91:4)**.

Keep me as the apple of Your eye; hide me under the shadow of Your wings. **(Psalm 17:8)**.

The sensation of being lifted reveals God's desire to elevate her spiritually, perhaps into her calling, her next season, or deeper understanding.

But those who wait on the Lord shall renew their strength; they shall mount up with wings like eagles…" **(Isaiah 40:31)**.

Math in School — Spiritual Wisdom and Divine Training

School represents a place of preparation, growth, and discipline. Math, specifically, reflects order, reasoning, logic, and structure. This tells us that God is bringing the dreamer (and you, the reader) into a season of spiritual learning. It's not about head knowledge alone, it's about divine understanding and the wisdom to rightly divide truth.

Get wisdom! Get understanding!... Wisdom is the principal thing; therefore, get wisdom. **(Proverbs 4:5,7)**.

Study to show yourself approved unto God, a worker who does not need to be ashamed. **(2 Timothy 2:15)**.

God Is Calling You Higher

This dream is not just for my daughter. It is for you, the one reading these words right now.

You may feel unseen or unsure of your spiritual identity. But the Holy Spirit recognizes those who reflect His image. Maybe you've been watching others who seem to carry a calling or mantle that you don't fully understand. But God is calling you to be still, to kneel, and to allow Him to wrap you in His Spirit.

You are being prepared. You are being covered. You are being called higher.

Don't resist the kneeling season—it leads to the lifting.
Don't fear the school season—it leads to wisdom.

Don't doubt the encounter, the Holy Spirit knows your name, your future, and your assignment.

Reflection for the Reader

Are you in a season of waiting, learning, or being hidden under God's wings?

Do you recognize the Holy Spirit's movement in the people around you?

Have you surrendered fully to God's divine covering and elevation?
Are you willing to let God "teach" you, even when the lessons are difficult?

Prayer:

Holy Spirit, I welcome You. Cover me with Your wings. Teach me to recognize Your movements in my life and in others. I kneel in surrender and invite Your presence to grip my heart, my shoulders, and my mind. Lift me where You want me to go. Train me in wisdom and understanding. I say yes to Your school, yes to Your Spirit, and yes to my divine calling. In Jesus' name, Amen.

Declarations:

I am seen and known by the Holy Spirit.

I kneel in surrender and rise in power.
I am covered by His wings and clothed in divine favor.

I am a student in God's school, and I will grow in wisdom and purpose.

Spirit is lifting me into my next season.

Spiritual Insights & Biblical Principles: The Hidden Work of the Holy Spirit

The Spirit Recognizes Spiritual Identity

In the dream, the colorful bird (symbolic of the Holy Spirit) was drawn to the girl who wore a coat that matched its feathers. This represents a deep truth: the Holy Spirit is drawn to those who walk in alignment with Him.

Your spiritual identity, your calling, character, purity, and obedience—acts like a spiritual garment.

But put on the Lord Jesus Christ and make no provision for the flesh. **(Romans 13:14).**

He has clothed me with the garments of salvation; He has covered me with the robe of righteousness. **(Isaiah 61:10).**

Principle: When you are clothed in righteousness, humility, and truth, the Spirit will rest upon you (Isaiah 11:2). God is drawn to spiritual resemblance.

Kneeling Comes Before Lifting

My daughter instinctively knelt when the bird came toward her. This act was not only humility, but spiritual readiness. In Scripture, kneeling often precedes divine encounters, angelic visits, or moments of transformation.

At the name of Jesus every knee should bow. **(Philippians 2:10).**

Humble yourselves in the sight of the Lord, and He will lift you up. **(James 4:10).**

This is a principle we cannot skip: before promotion comes posture.

Principle: Bowing in humility creates space for God's elevation. If you want to rise spiritually, you must first learn how to bow.

The Wings of the Spirit Are a Place of Safety and Power

The bird wrapping its wings around her is not only a symbol of protection, but of intimacy. God invites His children into the shadow of His wings—close enough to hear His heartbeat.

He shall cover you with His feathers, and under His wings you shall take refuge. **(Psalm 91:4)**.

You have been a shelter for me... I will abide in Your tabernacle forever; I will trust in the shelter of Your wings. **(Psalm 61:3–4)**. When God covers you, He is also preparing you. That intimate covering is also a hiding place for transformation.
Principle: God's wings are not just protection—they are preparation. Let Him hide you so He can shape you.

The School of the Spirit: Learning Before Leading
The transition from the spiritual moment to a school classroom doing math reveals a critical truth: God doesn't just anoint; He instructs. The Holy Spirit teaches, corrects, equips, and prepares us for divine assignments.

But the Helper, the Holy Spirit... will teach you all things. **(John 14:26)**.

It is good for a man to bear the yoke in his youth. **(Lamentations 3:27)**.

Let the wise hear and increase in learning, and the one who understands obtain guidance.
(Proverbs 1:5 ESV).

Math represents spiritual discipline—adding to your faith, multiplying wisdom, subtracting sin, and dividing truth rightly.

Principle: Before you can be used mightily by God, you must first become a student of His Spirit.

Elevation Is Coming—But Only at God's Timing

In the dream, it felt as though the bird was going to lift her. Yet, it didn't immediately fly away, it covered first, then prepared her through learning.

This is a message to the reader: don't rush the lifting. Wait for God's appointed time.

"To everything there is a season, a time for every purpose under heaven. **(Ecclesiastes 3:1)**.

"You saw me before I was born. Every day of my life was recorded in your book."
— **Psalm 139:16 (NLT)**

Principle: The covering comes before the calling, and the calling is shaped through quiet seasons of obedience.

The Holy Spirit is preparing a generation who wears the coat of His calling—those who will kneel before they rise, learn before they lead, and wait under His wings before they soar in power. Let this be your posture: clothed in His Spirit, bowed in humility, trained in wisdom, and ready to rise.

Awake in the Coffin

Dream Date: June 2025
Dream By Mother Stella

In the dream, my mother found herself inside a funeral home. She was lying in a coffin — dead — yet fully aware of everything happening around her. Though her body was lifeless, her spirit remained alert, observing every detail and presence in the room. Strangely, she was not alone. Next to her was another person also in a coffin — dead — but just like her, fully conscious and aware of everything going on.

They both remained still in their coffins, not moving or speaking, yet possessing a deep understanding of their surroundings. There was no fear, no confusion — only an overwhelming awareness while lying in what should have been the final resting place.

Spiritual Insight and Interpretation

(Continuation from June 2025 Dream)

This dream carries a weighty, prophetic message that speaks to the state of the soul, the condition of the church, and the urgent call to spiritual awakening in these last days. To be in a coffin — the symbol of death — and yet remain fully aware, reveals a divine paradox. It echoes the spiritual reality found in Scripture: that some appear dead on the outside, forgotten or hidden from man's view, yet are alive and awake in the Spirit, listening, watching, and discerning what others cannot.

Biblical Foundations of the Dream

Romans 6:11 (NKJV):
Likewise, you also, reckon yourselves to be dead indeed to sin, but alive to God in Christ Jesus our Lord.

What my mother experienced in this dream reflects the death of the flesh and the awakening of the spirit. Though she was in a coffin — representing the end of the natural man — she was spiritually alert. This mirrors Paul's teaching that we must die to sin, to self, to worldly distraction, in order to be alive to God. The death in the dream was not the end — it was a transition into awareness.

(Colossians 3:3 NKJV). For you died, and your life is hidden with Christ in God.

The Spirit of God is showing us a picture of what it means to live hidden in Christ. To the world, some of God's people may appear buried, forgotten, or spiritually silent — but they are hidden for a purpose, preserved by God, and fully aware in the Spirit.

The Funeral Home: The Sleeping Church

The setting of a funeral home is symbolic of the condition of many churches today. There is activity, ceremony, and appearance — yet spiritually, many lie in coffins: ritual without life, faith without fire, words without witness.

(Revelation 3:1-2 NKJV). You have a name that you are alive, but you are dead. Be watchful and strengthen the things which remain.

The message to Sardis is echoed in this dream. God is warning us that a name or a title is not life. Many in the body of Christ have maintained the outward shell of faith but have lost the vital presence of the Holy Spirit. Yet, just like in the dream, there remains awareness — a flicker of consciousness — and that is enough for God to send revival if we respond to His call.

Two in the Coffin – The Hidden Remnant

The presence of another person in a nearby coffin, also aware, points to a prophetic picture of the remnant — those who appear still, silent, or even gone — yet are positioned by God for a greater revealing.

Revelation 11:3 (NKJV):
"And I will give power to my two witnesses, and they will prophesy..."

This dream aligns with the role of God's hidden witnesses — those who may not be in pulpits or on stages, but who are watching, interceding, discerning, and waiting for God's appointed time. Like the witnesses of Revelation, they appear dead to the world, but they are empowered to speak life at God's command.

Ezekiel 37:12-14 (NKJV):
"Behold, O My people, I will open your graves and cause you to come up from your graves... I will put My Spirit in you, and you shall live."

This dream is also a resurrection prophecy — not just for individuals, but for the church at large. God is about to open the graves of His people — to bring back to life the forgotten, the hidden, the intercessors, the faithful ones who remained alert while the world thought they were finished.

Dear reader, could this dream be speaking to you? Perhaps you've been in a place that feels like a coffin — boxed in, still, without movement. Maybe people have looked at your situation and thought your story was over. Maybe even you have thought it.

But listen — the fact that you're aware, still listening, still seeking, means you are not dead. You are still spiritually alive, and that means God is not finished with you.

(John 11:25-26 NKJV). I am the resurrection and the life. He who believes in Me, though he may die, he shall live.

Jesus specializes in resurrection. Whether it's your joy, your purpose, your fire, or your faith — if it feels buried, God can bring it back to life.

Let this dream be a holy reminder that God sees the "still ones," the silent ones, the faithful ones who have died to the world but are alive in Him. It is not the loud who are always the living — sometimes, it's the quiet, watching ones who carry the greatest power.

Prayer of Awakening and Resurrection

Father God,
I thank You for speaking through dreams and visions in these last days. Just as You awakened my mother in that coffin, awaken every reader who feels buried, silenced, or forgotten. Let the grave clothes fall off. Let the Spirit of life rise up within them. Let them know that though they have died to the world, they are fully alive in You. Use them as witnesses in this hour, hidden but powerful, awake even in the silence.
In Jesus' mighty name, Amen.

The Sky Rolled Back

Dream By Son Eldrick – 2008

In a vivid dream my son Eldrick had back in 2008, he found himself in the middle of a vast, dry desert—barren and harsh. He was in full military gear, stationed with fellow soldiers on one side of a river, while another opposing military force stood across from them. The two sides were engaged in combat, face-to-face in the midst of warfare. The environment was tense, fierce, and urgent.

Then something beyond comprehension took place.

Suddenly, the sky began to roll back like a scroll—just as described in **(Revelation 6:14):**"Then the sky receded as a scroll when it is rolled up, and every mountain and island was moved out of its place."

From the heavens came a powerful procession of angels, each one sounding a brown shofar—earth-toned and ancient in appearance. These heavenly trumpets thundered across the sky, signaling the arrival of a King. The brown color symbolized humility and the voice of God calling from heaven to earth **(Numbers 10:9; Joel 2:1)**.

Then Eldrick saw Jesus!

The Lord was riding with a great army—radiant, majestic, and fierce in glory. He descended from the heavens with power and authority, surrounded by angelic hosts dressed in white. It was the vision of Christ returning as the

Commander of Heaven's Army, as foretold in (**Revelation 19:11–14**).

"Now I saw heaven opened, and behold, a white horse. And He who sat on him was called Faithful and True... and the armies in heaven, clothed in fine linen, white and clean, followed Him on white horses."

At the sight of Jesus, Eldrick dropped his weapon and fell to his knees in total surrender. His hands rose in prayer, his heart overwhelmed by awe and holy fear. One of his fellow soldiers shouted, "What are you doing? You're going to get yourself killed!"

But when his comrade looked up and saw the skies torn open, the angels, the trumpet blasts, and Jesus Himself, he

too dropped to his knees in reverence beside Eldrick. Then the dream ended.

Spiritual Insights: A Glimpse of Armageddon

As Eldrick shared this dream, I was reminded immediately of Armageddon—the prophesied final battle between the forces of heaven and the armies of darkness (Revelation 16:14–16). The desert battlefield in his dream reflects the spiritual landscape of the end times: dry, hostile, and divided between the righteous and the rebellious.

The river between the two armies symbolized the divide between truth and deception, the holy and the profane. The brown shofars were not merely instruments, but heavenly warnings—sounding the arrival of the King of Kings. As in (**Joel 2:1**):"Blow the trumpet in Zion, and sound an alarm in My holy mountain! Let all the inhabitants of the land tremble; for the day of the Lord is coming, for it is at hand."

This dream carries the weight of Revelation. It is a prophetic call to all who are caught in the battle: choose your side. As in Armageddon, there will be no neutrality. All must decide whether to fight with worldly weapons—or fall in surrender before Christ, the eternal Victor.

Dear reader, this dream is not just for Eldrick. It is for you.

The spiritual battle is already raging. You may feel warfare in your home, your mind, or your spirit. But take heart—Jesus is not distant. He is coming again. And every eye will see Him. Every knee will bow **(Philippians 2:10-11).**

Will you be found holding onto your own strength? Or will you be like Eldrick, laying down your weapons and lifting your hands to the One who saves?

Prayer

Father in Heaven,
We thank You for dreams and visions that awaken our spirits to eternal realities. Thank You for reminding us that we are living in the last days, and that Your return is near. Just as You opened the sky in Eldrick's dream, open the heavens over our hearts and homes.

Lord, we lay down every carnal weapon. We surrender our fears, our pride, and our false strength. Let us be found ready when the shofar sounds. May we stand with You in the final battle—not by power, not by might, but by Your Spirit.

In the name of Jesus Christ, our returning King, Amen.

Prophetic Decree

I decree that I will not fear the battle, for the Lord goes before me.
I decree that my heart will be alert, awake, and surrendered when the trumpet of God sounds.
I decree that I am on the Lord's side and sealed by His blood.
I decree that the armies of heaven are greater than the armies of earth.
I decree that Jesus is coming back, and I will be ready kneeling, worshiping, and watching.

Even so, come Lord Jesus. Amen.

The Anointed Outpouring Over My Family

Dream Date: Summer of 1999

It was the summer of 1999, and the day in my dream was exceedingly bright, as though the heavens themselves were declaring the glory of God (Psalm 19:1). I stood outside with my beloved mother and my four children. Together, we lifted our eyes toward the sky, sensing something divine was about to unfold. The atmosphere was still yet filled with holy anticipation.

As we gazed upward, our eyes were met with a sight that filled us with both awe and reverence—a colossal angel stretched across the entire sky. This heavenly being was majestic beyond words, with long, curly hair flowing like waves of light. Around its waist was a golden sash, glistening with righteousness and authority (Revelation 1:13). But what caught our attention most was the object it held in its hands—a breathtakingly beautiful and massive golden cup.

The cup was adorned with intricate carvings and grave etchings, as if it held not just oil, but purpose, destiny, and sanctification. The top of the cup radiated light, and within it was oil—pure and shining, as if refined by fire. The angel lifted this divine vessel with holy intention, and before us, began to pour the oil out across the entire sky. It wasn't just falling—it was being released, directed over our family like a sacred covering **(Joel 2:28-29)**.

Then the angel did something profound. With tender might, she turned her head and swept it across the sky, as if washing or wiping the oil over us—an anointing unlike any I had known. I sensed that the oil was not just a symbol of consecration, but of God's Spirit being poured out over me, my mother, and my children. As the oil covered the heavens, I felt it fall upon our lives, our futures, and generations yet unborn. And then—I awoke.

Dear reader, this dream was not only for me—it is also for you. The angel with the cup of oil speaks to the outpouring of the Holy Spirit upon families in these last days. The oil represents anointing, healing, sanctification, and divine protection. The fact that the angel poured it over the sky and intentionally wiped it upon us reveals God's desire to cover His people from above, from heaven itself.

This vision is a powerful reminder of the promise in (**Isaiah 44:3 NKJV**).

For I will pour water on him who is thirsty, and floods on the dry ground; I will pour My Spirit on your descendants, and My blessing on your offspring.

And again in **(Acts 2:17 NKJV)**. And it shall come to pass in the last days, says God, that I will pour out of My Spirit on all flesh; your sons and your daughters shall prophesy.

This dream assures us that God sees our families. He is still anointing households, breaking generational curses, and preparing His people for His divine work. The sky being covered in oil is a heavenly declaration that what God is doing is not hidden but made manifest to those who have eyes to see and ears to hear (Matthew 13:16).

Heavenly Father,
Thank You for the gift of dreams, visions, and divine encounters. Lord, I lift up every reader right now—mothers, fathers, children, and generations. Pour out Your oil upon them, just as You did in this vision. Let the anointing break every yoke, heal every wound, and seal every promise spoken over their lives.

Cover their skies, Lord. Let Your Spirit saturate their homes, their hearts, and their futures. Just as You anointed me and my family in this dream, I pray that every household reading these words would receive Your holy outpouring. May they walk in boldness, protection, and sanctification, under the shadow of Your mighty wings.
In the powerful name of Jesus Christ,
Amen.

The Weight and Wonder of the Oil

As I stood under that sacred sky, watching the angel pour the oil, I felt a shift in the atmosphere. The brightness of the day seemed to glow even brighter—not from the sun, but from the light of heaven itself. A holy stillness surrounded us. It was as if time paused. The angel's presence did not stir fear—it brought peace, reverence, and awe. The oil flowed slowly, not like rain, but like a gentle river from the cup of glory, stretching across the heavens like golden threads of divine grace.

I looked at my mother—her eyes lifted upward, glistening with tears. My children stood still, caught in holy wonder. I sensed in that moment that this was not just about our earthly lives, but about the generations that would come through us. It was as though God was marking our family for something sacred. The oil carried weight was not just oil, but the presence of the Holy Spirit being released upon us.

The angel's sweeping motion across the sky wasn't random; it was deliberate—like a priest anointing the altar, or a scribe sealing a scroll. The covering over us was total. I felt something in my spirit stir—a call, a commissioning, a sanctifying grace. The oil spoke without words: "You are chosen, you are covered, you are called."

I didn't speak a word, but my heart cried out, "Lord, let this oil remain." I sensed that God was sealing my household with purpose. The angel didn't speak, but I understood everything. The oil was a symbol of divine assignment, of protection from what was to come, and of the Spirit's work to be done through our family **(Zechariah 4:6)**.

Dear reader, I believe this same oil is being poured out upon you, your home, your children, and your destiny. This dream is a call to receive the anointing, walk in the covering, and stand under the open heavens. The angel's actions remind us of (**Psalm 133:2 NKJV**).

It is like the precious oil upon the head, running down on the beard, the beard of Aaron, running down on the edge of his garments.

This oil was not for one moment—it was for legacy. For your ministry. For the battles you will face. For the promises God has spoken that have yet to manifest.

The Lord is pouring out oil not just for healing, but for commissioning—to raise you up, to raise your children, and to sanctify your bloodline for the glory of His kingdom.

Today, I declare over you, dear reader, that the oil of God is not withheld. Lift your eyes. Believe the outpouring. The same God who poured oil from heaven over me and my family is ready to release it over you.

Declare in faith:

"Lord, I receive the oil. Anoint my life, anoint my family, and let Your presence cover my home. Let every generational curse be broken and let generational blessings flow like oil from heaven." Let the oil flow. Let your heart be still. Let your soul receive.

The Two Generals and the Spirit Behind Power

Vision Date: January 21,2025

As I was lying in my bed early that morning, I entered into prayer, seeking the Lord with a quiet heart. While in prayer, a vivid and intense vision opened before me—one that stirred my spirit with great urgency.

In the vision, I saw the White House standing firm and still. It was a quiet but heavy scene, as if something divine and serious was taking place behind the veil of the natural. In front of the White House stood two generals—strong, dignified men of authority. They were not moving but stood at a distance, fully attentive, their eyes fixed toward the White House. Their posture spoke of high command, alertness, and great responsibility, as if they were guardians or watchmen set in place for a purpose.

But suddenly, my attention was drawn behind one of the generals. There, standing ominously, was a raging demon. Its presence was fierce—full of wrath, unrest, and spiritual aggression. Yet the general did not seem to see or feel it. He remained fixed in place, unaware of the evil presence behind him. The demon loomed as if it had influence or was assigned to interfere, manipulate, or whisper into leadership.

"For we wrestle not against flesh and blood, but against principalities, against powers, against the rulers of the darkness of this world, against spiritual wickedness in high places." — **Ephesians 6:12 (KJV).**

This vision was a revelation of spiritual warfare at the highest levels. The two generals represented leaders—men of authority who are positioned in natural power, yet potentially vulnerable to spiritual influence. One appeared to stand

159

alone, but the other had a dark spirit working behind him—an unseen force that sought to direct decisions and influence outcomes without detection.

It reminded me of Daniel's vision and prayer when the angel of the Lord was delayed because of the demonic principality over Persia. Only through angelic warfare did the breakthrough come **(Daniel 10:12–13)**. This shows us that behind earthly power, there is always a spiritual reality, either led by truth or manipulated by darkness.

The prudent man foresees the evil, and hideth himself: but the simple pass on, and are punished. **(Proverbs 27:12 KJV)**.

What appeared orderly and powerful on the surface held hidden spiritual conflict beneath. This vision is a call to the saints—not to fear—but to discern, to watch, and to pray. It is not enough to look at leadership in the natural. We must ask: Who stands behind them? What spirit is at work in their counsel?

Spiritual Reflection for the Reader:

Dear reader, this vision is not political, it is prophetic. The Lord is opening the eyes of His people to see beyond appearances. Two men can look equally positioned in power, but only the Spirit can reveal who is being influenced from behind.

Let this vision stir you to deeper intercession. Pray for righteous leaders. Pray that deception and demonic voices be silenced. Pray that those called to leadership would be guarded by the Spirit of the Living God and not misled by unclean spirits.

"Be sober, be vigilant; because your adversary the devil, as a roaring lion, walketh about, seeking whom he may devour. (**1 Peter 5:8 KJV**).

May this serve as a call to take your post in the Spirit. Be a watchman on the wall. Be a voice crying out for the unveiling of truth, and for the light of Christ to expose and cast out every dark influence at work behind leadership.

Continuing Vision Insight: What Lies Behind Authority

This vision of the two generals standing before the White House is a prophetic unveiling—a glimpse behind the curtain of natural leadership into the reality of spiritual influence. One general stood alone. The other, though seemingly strong and noble, had a raging demon behind him—hidden, yet active. This is a sobering revelation: not every person in power is operating solely from their own wisdom or strength.

Throughout Scripture, we see examples where leaders were either guided by the Spirit of God or influenced by the enemy.

King Saul, once anointed, began to be tormented by an evil spirit **(1 Samuel 16:14)**. Though still in position, his decisions began to reflect the chaos of demonic influence.

Judas Iscariot, one of the twelve, walked with Jesus—yet the Bible says, "Then entered Satan into Judas…" **(Luke 22:3)**. He looked like the others, but something had entered behind the scenes.

This vision confirms that in today's time, spiritual warfare is not reserved for churches alone—it is operating in places of power, in government, in institutions, and even among those who carry military or political authority. The two generals symbolize a divine contrast: one untouched, the other under siege from a demonic force.

Surely the Lord God will do nothing, but He revealed His secret unto His servants the prophets. (**Amos 3:7**).

This is why the Lord revealed this to you—not to create fear, but to awaken the Church to pray with eyes open and discernment sharp. We must not pray based only on what we see or hear in the news; we must pray based on what is revealed in the Spirit. If there are demons influencing our leaders, then our intercession must match the intensity of the battle

Spiritual Symbolism from Vision

The White House: A symbol of national power, law, and influence over multitudes.

The Two Generals: High-ranking authority figures. One represents a vessel of neutrality or righteousness. The other, though respected in the natural, is under unseen spiritual warfare.

The Raging Demon: Represents chaos, deception, control, and hidden influence—particularly from principalities assigned to deceive rulers and guide them into decisions that oppose God's will.

This matches the pattern of Daniel 10, where Daniel fasted and prayed, and the angel who came to deliver the answer explained how demonic forces in the heavens resisted him:

But the prince of the kingdom of Persia withstood me one and twenty days. (**Daniel 10:13**). Some breakthroughs in leadership will not happen without intense spiritual warfare and intercessory prayer.

A Call to the Reader: Watch, Discern, and Intercede

Beloved reader, you are not powerless in this hour. You are called to watch, to discern, and to intercede. There are times when the Lord allows us to see spiritual activity so that we may war against it—not in the flesh, but by the authority of Jesus Christ.

The effectual fervent prayer of a righteous man availed much. (**James 5:16 KJV**).

Your prayers matter. Your intercession can be the tipping point for angelic intervention. This is the hour for the Body of Christ to rise, not with carnal weapons, but with the Word of God, the power of the Holy Spirit, and the authority given to us through the blood of Jesus.

Prayer of Intercession and Discernment

Heavenly Father,
We come before You with humble hearts, thanking You for revealing the hidden things. Thank You for unveiling the truth behind earthly power so that we may stand in our rightful place as intercessors. We pray now for every leader, especially those in positions of governmental and military authority.

Expose every demonic presence influencing leadership. Tear down every high thing that exalts itself against the knowledge of God. Let Your light shine into dark places and remove every counsel of the enemy from around those called to lead.

Lord, station angels around our leaders who seek righteousness. Remove those who serve darkness and elevate those who seek Your heart. Give the Church spiritual eyes to see and a heart to pray fervently.

We declare Your Word: "No weapon formed against us shall prosper." We stand on Your promise that "when the enemy comes in like a flood, the Spirit of the Lord shall lift up a standard against him."

We raise that standard now—in our homes, our cities, and over this nation. In Jesus' mighty name,
Amen.

Do You Know What You Think You Know?

Dream Date Year: 2023

In 2023, I had a dream that stirred my spirit to its core. It wasn't long or dramatic, but it carried the weight of eternal significance. In the dream, I heard a voice—not ordinary, but with power and spiritual authority—ask me a profound question:
"Do you know what you think you know?"

Immediately, I awoke, my heart stirred and my spirit alert. I felt the presence of God in the room, and I began to pray. I asked, "Lord, what are you showing me? What would You have me do with this question?" For two years, I pondered this moment. The question lingered, never fading. It was not something to shrug off or forget—it demanded reflection, action, and obedience. I believe now that the Lord was not only awakening me, but also calling me to awaken others. And so, two years later, I am writing this not just for myself, but for you, dear reader.

Spiritual Insight: A Call to Self-Examination

The question, "Do you know what you think you know?" is more than rhetorical. It is spiritual. It challenges us to evaluate our faith, our beliefs, and our understanding of God, His Word, and His will. In the times we live in, many believe they are walking in truth, but the truth is not just what we believe—it is what aligns with the Word of God and the Spirit of Truth.

Jesus said in **(John 8:32),**"Then you will know the truth, and the truth will set you free. "But how can we know the truth if we are not willing to examine what we think we know?

In **(Proverbs 14:12),** we are warned: There is a way that seems right to a man, but its end is the way of death.

This verse reminds us that not everything we believe or assume is right, just because it feels or seems right. We must humble ourselves before God and allow the Holy Spirit to search our hearts and correct our understanding.

Biblical Reflections and Warnings

The Pharisees Thought They Knew

The religious leaders in Jesus' day thought they knew the Scriptures, but they missed the Messiah standing right before them. Jesus said to them in **(John 5:39-40),**"You study the Scriptures diligently because you think that in them you have eternal life. These are the very Scriptures that testify about Me, yet you refuse to come to Me to have life.

Paul's Transformation

Before he became the Apostle Paul, Saul was zealous for God—but wrong in his knowledge. He persecuted the very Church that Christ died for, believing he was doing God's will. It wasn't until his encounter with Jesus on the road to Damascus that he was truly awakened. **(Acts 9:4-5)** records this moment: "Saul, Saul, why do you persecute Me? "Who are you, Lord?" Saul asked."

Saul thought he knew—but he didn't. This shows us how dangerous it is to operate in spiritual ignorance while believing we are right.

Revelation for the Reader

To the reader, I ask you to answer this question:
"Do you know what you think you know?"
Has your understanding of God, salvation, holiness, or righteousness been shaped more by culture, tradition, or personal experience than by the Word of God and the leading of the Holy Spirit?

We are living in a time where deception is rampant, and truth is under attack. Jesus warned us in Matthew 24:4-5, "Watch out that no one deceives you. For many will come in My name, claiming, 'I am the Messiah,' and will deceive many."

Deception works by twisting what we think we know. This is why God is calling us back to intimacy with His Word and with His Spirit. The Holy Spirit is our teacher and guide (John 14:26), and only through His illumination can we discern truth from error.

Call to Action

Test What You Believe

Compare everything you believe with Scripture. Ask the Holy Spirit to reveal any falsehood or assumptions. **(1 John 4:1 says),** "Dear friends, do not believe every spirit, but test the spirits to see whether they are from God."

Stay Humble and Teachable

No matter how long you've walked with God, there's always more to learn. Proverbs 3:5-6 urge us, "Trust in the Lord with all your heart and lean not on your own understanding."

Return to the Feet of Jesus

Let your theology be birthed from relationship with Him, not religion. Sit at His feet like Mary did (Luke 10:39) and let Him speak truth into your spirit.

A Closing Prayer for You

Heavenly Father,
I thank You for the one reading this message. I pray that Your Spirit would gently and powerfully stir their heart, just as You stirred mine. Lord, we confess that sometimes we walk in what we think is truth, but it is not always aligned with You. We humbly ask You to reveal what we have misunderstood, to correct what is in error, and to fill us with discernment and wisdom from above.

Open the eyes of our understanding, that we may know You more deeply. Teach us to walk in humility, always seeking Your heart above our opinions. Father, protect us from deception and pride, and let Your truth be the anchor of our souls.

Holy Spirit, leads us into all truth. Let us not rely on what we think we know, but rather on what You reveal in Your Word and through Your Spirit. Let us grow in grace, in wisdom, and in fear of the Lord. May we become people of truth, fully surrendered to the will of the Father. In Jesus' mighty name, Amen.

Devotional Reflection

Do You Know What You Think You Know?

Scripture Focus:
"Examine yourselves, to see whether you are in the faith. Test yourselves."(**2 Corinthians 13:5, ESV**)

Devotion

There is a weight to the question: "Do you know what you think you know?" It calls us out of spiritual assumption and into holy awareness. Many of us walk with beliefs passed down from culture, tradition, or emotion—without ever truly testing them in the light of God's Word.

Today, the Holy Spirit is extending a gentle but urgent invitation:
Examine your heart.
Question your assumptions.
Revisit your foundations.
Are you standing on truth, or on a mixture of truth and man's opinions?

In a time of increasing deception, we must anchor ourselves in God's unchanging Word. The Bereans were commended in Acts 17:11 because they "examined the Scriptures every day to see if what Paul said was true." If they tested even Apostle Paul, how much more should we test what we have always believed?

This is not a call to doubt God—but to doubt the flesh, to lay down pride, and to be teachable in the hands of the Master. Jesus promised that the Holy Spirit would lead us into all truth **(John 16:13)**. But we must be willing to follow Him—even if it means unlearning some things.

Meditation Questions

1. What are some things you believe about God, faith, or the world that you have never tested with Scripture?

2. Have you ever had to unlearn something that you once thought was true? How did God lead you through that?

3. Are you willing to let go of your opinion if the Holy Spirit reveals it does not align with His Word?

Scriptures for Deeper Study

(Proverbs 3:5-7). Trust in the Lord... and lean not on your own understanding.

(2 Timothy 2:15). Study to show yourself approved unto God.

(John 14:26). The Holy Spirit will teach you all things.

(Isaiah 55:8-9). My thoughts are not your thoughts.

(Psalm 139:23-24). Search me, O God, and know my heart.

Father God,
I come before You today humbly. I lay down my pride, my opinions, and my assumptions. If there is anything I believe that is not of You, show me. If there is anything I have clung to in my own understanding, forgive me. I invite Your Holy Spirit to be my teacher, my guide, and my light.

Search my heart, O God, and lead me in the way everlasting. Help me to love truth more than comfort. Let Your Word be the foundation I stand on, and not the opinions of men. Lord, I surrender my thoughts and ask You to shape my mind and heart into Your likeness.
Jesus, you are the Way, the Truth, and the Life. Help me to walk in You fully. In Your name I pray. Amen.

Acknowledgments

I would like to acknowledge and honor my dear mother, Stella, whose love and wisdom have been a guiding light in my life. To my beloved children — Maria, Travis, Eldrick, and Louis — you are my heart and my strength. I also extend my love to my precious grandchildren and my daughters-in-laws, future Son-in-Law and to all my loving family and friends. The lord told my dear mother in a dream we are the most preaching, gospel singing and praying family "In the World". Keep your eyes focus on our Lord Jesus Christ.

May the Lord continue to bless each of you richly. I pray that you remain steadfast in your hunger for the Word of God. Read your Bibles continually, walk in faith, and never stop seeking the Lord. Teach your children — and your children's children — to love and serve the Lord with all their heart, soul, and mind.

May your lives be a living testimony of God's grace and may generations after you rise up in faith and obedience to His Word.

With all my love and prayers,

Donna Lisa Davis

Author

Donna Lisa Davis

Ever since childhood, I knew there was something different about me—a quiet awareness that I was called to surrender fully to the Lord Jesus Christ. Even as a little girl, the Lord began revealing Himself to me through prophetic dreams. At the age of sixteen, I began to understand that these dreams were not just imagination, they were divine messages from Heaven. As I opened the pages of the Bible, my dreams came to life before my eyes, and I knew without a doubt that God was speaking.

Acts 2:17 says, "In the last days, saith God, I will pour out of my Spirit upon all flesh: and your sons and your daughters shall prophesy, and your young men shall see visions, and your old men shall dream dreams." This verse became a mirror to my journey. It gave language to what I was experiencing and confirmed the calling placed on my life.

I thank the Lord for His grace—for guiding me, for covering me in times of confusion and sin, and for never letting me go. His hand was always upon me, even when I didn't fully understand His plan.

It is my prayer that this book touches hearts and awakens spirits. May it stir a holy hunger in readers to open their Holy Bibles and encounter the living God for themselves. May they see His love, hear His voice, and know that He is calling them too.

To God be the glory.

Author Quote:

"The Lord spoke to me through dreams, and the Word confirmed it. I write not to be seen, but so that others might see Him." – Donna Lisa Davis